ANTIQUE JEWELRY

with prices

Doris J. Snell

Cover design: Heather Miller
Photographs: Charles Gehret Studio

Library of Congress Catalog
Card Number 81-52173

ISBN 0-87069-369-7

Published by

580 Water's Edge Road
Lombard, Illinois 60148

This book is dedicated to my husband Robert and my niece Diana Karas. It is also written in memory of my son Alexander, my parents Alexander and Louise Karas, and Byron Haverly-Blackford.

Acknowledgments

Thank you Don Brown, Acquisitions Editor, and Jim Leimkuhler, General Manager, of the Wallace-Homestead Book Company for affording me the opportunity to write this book.

The Charles Gehret Studios in Steelton, Pennsylvania, produced all of the photographs and we are grateful for their professional services.

Many beautiful examples of antique jewelry were loaned so they could be photographed for this price guide. Thank you Rose Marie Salter, Camp Hill, Pennsylvania, and Jane-Paul Antiques of Harrisburg for the very special assistance you gave me. I will always be appreciative.

Robert E. Tarner, manager of Rose Marie's Antiques in Camp Hill provided invaluable aid dating certain pieces and identifying their composition. I will remember his kindness and sincerity.

Other help was given by Susan Edwards, graduate student at Yale University and my patient husband, Robert. Without their affection, understanding, and inspiration this book would never have materialized.

Contents

Acknowledgments 4

Introduction 6

Bracelets 7

Brooches and Pins 21

Cameo Jewelry 46

Chains and Watches 53

Earrings 60

Fobs and Emblem Charms 64

Garnet Jewelry 82

Lavaliers, Lockets, Necklaces, and Pendants 85

Miscellaneous 105

Mourning Jewelry 107

Rings 112

Bibliography 122

Index 125

About the Author 128

Introduction

This guide was compiled to provide the reader with realistic retail values for the types of antique and collectible jewelry currently offered for sale in various antiques stores throughout the country. Examples of museum-quality pieces were deliberately excluded, because the scarcity of such pieces would make their value of academic interest, only.

Antique Jewelry with Prices is a practical, easy-to-use book that is, for the most part, divided into sections according to items, i.e., bracelets, pendants, rings, etc. Each piece illustrated is throughly identified, dated, and priced. An inclusive Index containing each individual item will be found at the back of the book.

For those interested in shell cameos (carved from seashells) it is helpful to be able to distinguish each type by its distinctive color. When carved, cornelian shell produces a creamy face on a reddish brown background. Sardonyx shell produces a white face on a brown background, and rosalyn shell produces a white face on a pink background.

Please note the spelling of the word cornelian in this book. It took many years, and finally a trip to Italy, for me to obtain a comprehensive understanding of shell cameos. The spelling "cornelian" as opposed to "carnelian" is believed to be the more accurate.

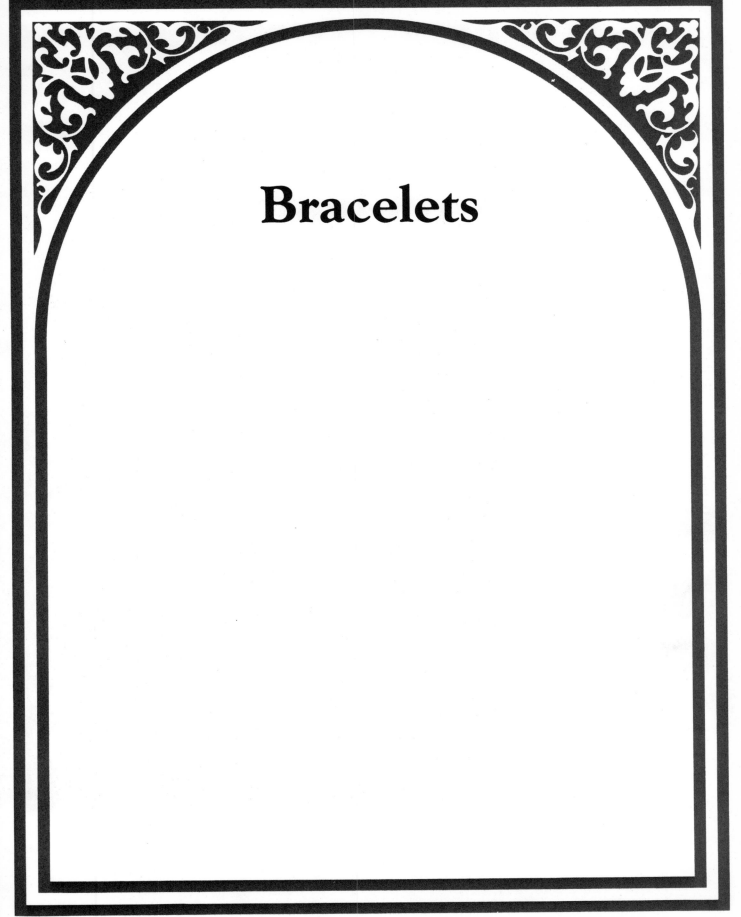

Bracelets

Scotch agate links,
rolled gold trim
$275

Garnets set in
rolled gold plate
$125

Garnets,
rolled gold plate
$375

Gold filled
$185

Less than 10k gold,
ruby
$175

Gold filled
$125

Bride's bracelet,
garnets, gold filled
$155

Bride's bracelet,
garnets, gold filled
$155

Gold filled,
black enameling
$90

Assorted bracelets, circa 1860–1890.

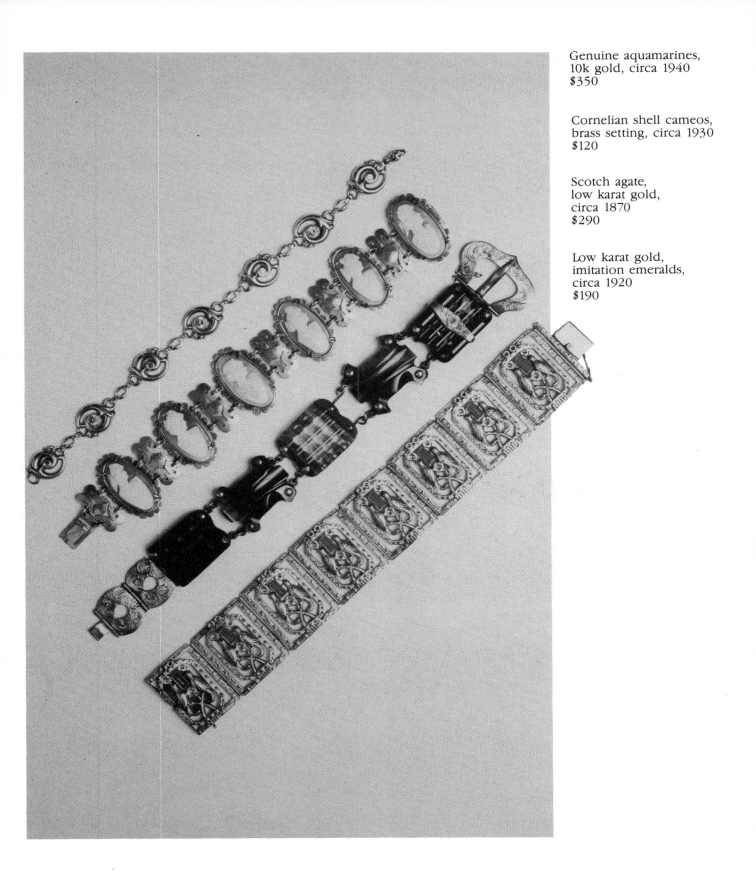

Genuine aquamarines,
10k gold, circa 1940
$350

Cornelian shell cameos,
brass setting, circa 1930
$120

Scotch agate,
low karat gold,
circa 1870
$290

Low karat gold,
imitation emeralds,
circa 1920
$190

These four bracelets show style changes that took place from Victorian to modern days.

Engraved, ½″ width,
$90

Engraved ⅜″ width
$85

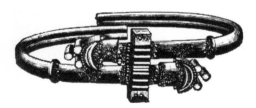

Engraved, ¼″ width,
$85

Engraved, ¼″ width
$85

Ornamented,
$90

Garnets and pearls,
$175

Ornamented,
$90

Ornamented,
$110

Ornamented,
$110

Ornamented,
$110

Bracelets, circa 1889, all rolled gold plate.

10

$50

$50

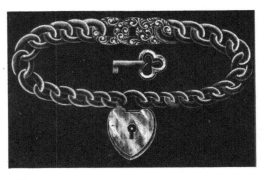

$60

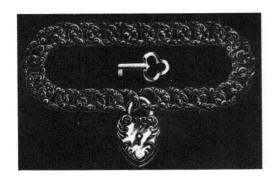

$70

$70

$70

$55

$65

Gold-filled bracelets, circa 1896.

Rose gold filled,
coral cameo
$150

Rose gold filled,
rhinestone in mouth
$165

Sterling silver,
gray finish
$65

$75

Four amethysts,
two rhinestones
$125

Pearl, eight sapphires,
six rhinestones, each side
$90

$65

$110

Sterling silver
$80

Bracelets, circa 1917, yellow gold filled
unless otherwise identified.

Frosted crystal and brilliants
$42

Brilliants and imitation crystal
(exact copy of a platinum and diamond bracelet)
$40

Imitation blue sapphires and brilliants
$35

Imitation peridot
$35

Imitation amethysts
$35

Sterling with rhodium finish,
imitation onyx, brilliants
$35

Imitation blue sapphires and brilliants
$30

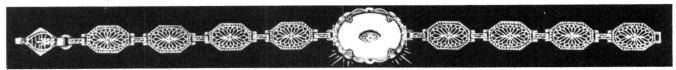

Sterling silver with rhodium finish,
frosted crystal, and brilliants
$30

Rose-colored glass stones
$30

Bracelets, circa 1932, rhodium mountings,
except where indicated.

13

Imitation emerald and brilliants
$55

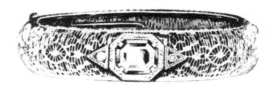

Crystal and brilliants
$49

Brilliants
$46

Frosted crystal and brilliants
$46

Rhodium, frosted crystal,
and brilliants
$46

Sterling with chrome finish,
imitation sapphires
$45

Sterling with chrome finish,
brilliants
$45

White gold plate,
imitation blue sapphires
$37

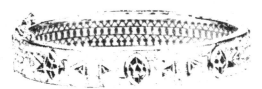

White gold plate
imitation blue sapphires, and
brilliants
$37

Rhodium with imitation
emerald baguettes
$35

Rhodium with crystal baguettes
$35

Chrome, pink glass stones
and brilliants
$34

Bracelets, circa 1932, rhodium mountings,
except where indicated.

14

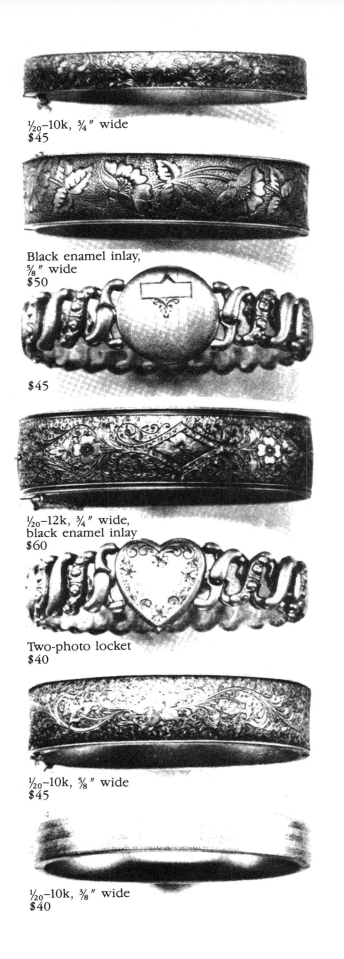

½₀-10k, ¾″ wide
$45

Black enamel inlay,
⅝″ wide
$50

$45

½₀-12k, ¾″ wide,
black enamel inlay
$60

Two-photo locket
$40

½₀-10k, ⅝″ wide
$45

½₀-10k, ⅜″ wide
$40

Sterling silver, ½″ wide
$70

Sterling silver,
⅝″ wide
$75

½₀-12k, ⅝″ wide
$85

$85

½₀-12k, ½″ wide
$50

½₀-12k, ⅜″ wide,
woven mesh, two-photo locket
$110

½₀-12k, ½″ wide,
woven mesh, two-photo locket
$110

Bracelets, circa 1940, yellow gold filled,
except where indicated.

15

Woven mesh
$70

Woven mesh
$60

Woven mesh
$90

Woven mesh, simulated pearl,
black enamel inlay
$80

Plain and engraved links
$55

Gold filled green leaves,
gold filled red flowers
$50

Gold filled red and green flowers
$50

Gold filled green leaves,
gold filled red flowers
$50

Plain and engraved links
$45

Bracelets, circa 1941, all yellow gold filled.

Red and green gold filled
$40

Black onyx, diamond
$50

Red and green gold filled
$45

Cornelian cameo
$75

Red and green gold filled
$40

Cuff-style bracelets, circa 1941, gold filled.

$40

Mother of pearl set with cameo
$55

Oynx,
genuine cultured pearl
$40

$40

$40

Green gold inlay
$40

Red and green gold inlay
$40

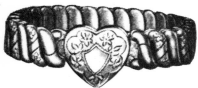

Cameo
$55

Green gold inlay
$40

Red and green gold inlay
$35

$35

Red and green gold overlay
$40

$40

Bracelets and lockets, circa 1942, yellow gold
filled.

18

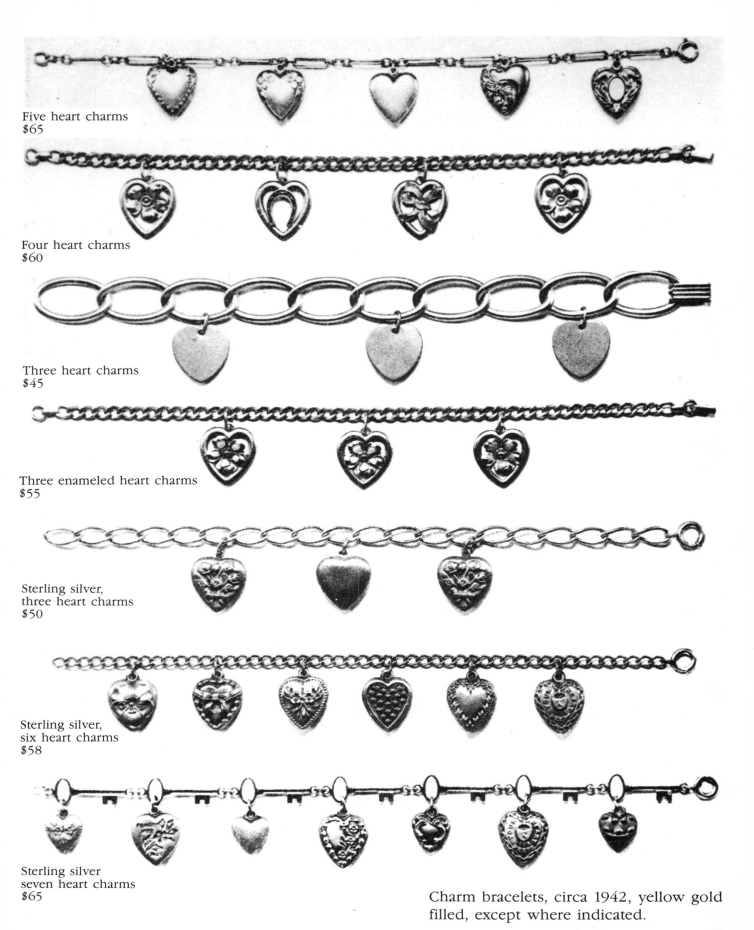

Five heart charms
$65

Four heart charms
$60

Three heart charms
$45

Three enameled heart charms
$55

Sterling silver,
three heart charms
$50

Sterling silver,
six heart charms
$58

Sterling silver
seven heart charms
$65

Charm bracelets, circa 1942, yellow gold filled, except where indicated.

Three imitation zircons
$65

Three genuine carved jade stones
$80

Three rose diamonds in genuine black onyx
$95

Three cornelian shell cameos
$69

Cornelian shell cameo
$65

Two-tone finish,
three zircons
$60

Sterling, five genuine zircons
$50

Genuine zircon
$45

Two-tone finish,
eight cultured pearls
$45

Bracelets, circa 1943, yellow gold filled,
except where indicated.

20

Brooches and Pins

$75

$75

$65

$60

$70

$85

$125

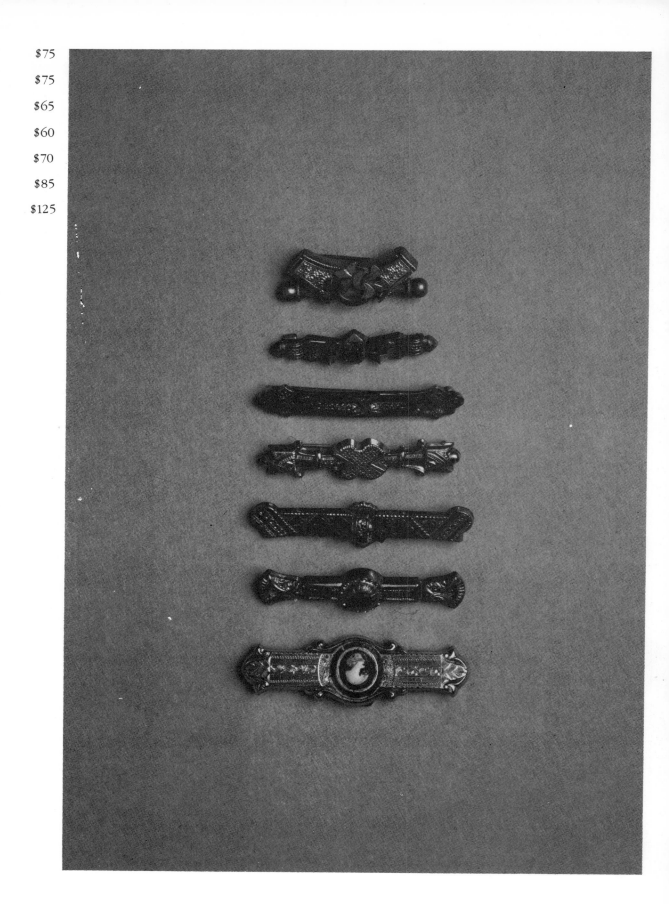

Bar pins, circa 1870–1900. Fronts are rolled
gold; backs are brass.

22

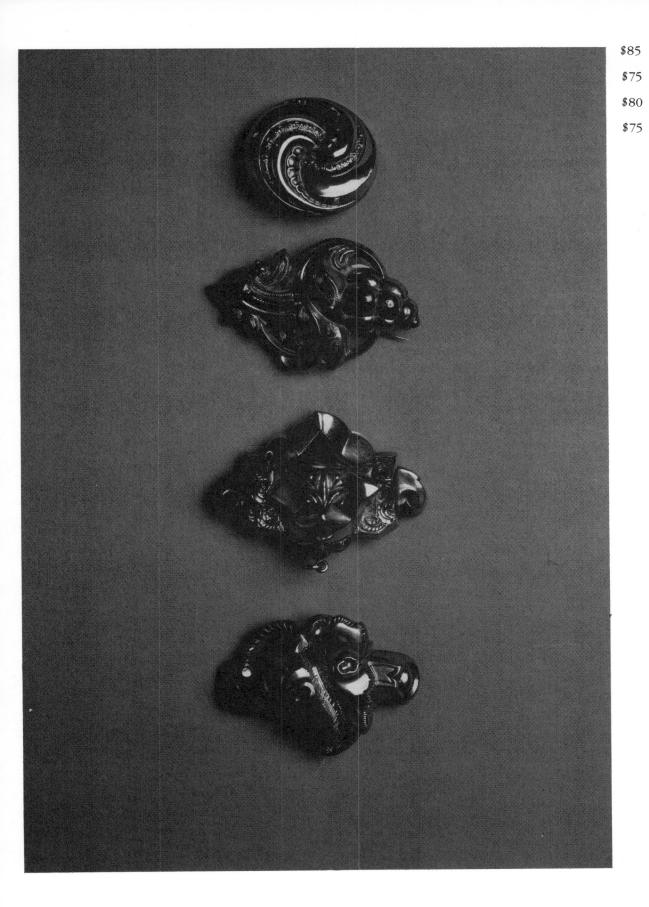

$85

$75

$80

$75

Victorian hollowware brooches, circa
1860–1880, have low karat gold fronts.

23

Brooch,
gold filled, painting on
porcelain,
$95

Chatelaine (watch) pin,
gold filled,
$90

Chatelaine (watch) pin,
14k gold,
$175

Chatelaine (watch) pin,
gold,
$190

Chatelaine (watch) pin,
gold filled, garnet
$70

Chatelaine (watch) pin,
gold
$175

Gold front, garnet
$95

Gold front, applied design
$95

Gold front
$95

Gold, garnets
$180

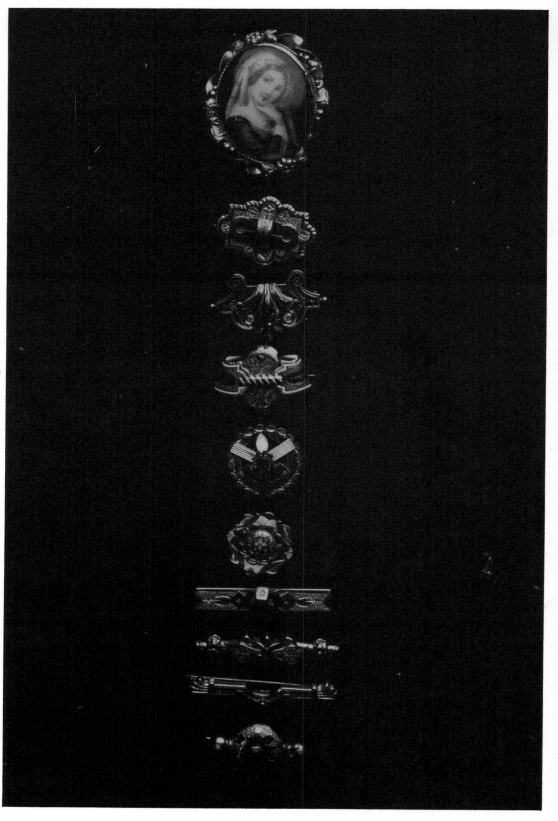

Brooches and pins, circa 1880–1900.

Lava cameo,
low karat gold setting,
$295

Intaglio,
low karat gold setting,
$125

Human hair,
14k findings,
$175

Brooches and cross, circa 1870–1890.

1840–1850
Painting on porcelain
$125

Pre-1840
Artist signed painting, reset in late 1800s
in a brass back with marcasites on upper border
$375

1870–1890
Mosaic in low karat gold setting
$190

$45

$60 $45

$45

Brooches, circa 1900–1920, handpainted
porcelain with brass settings or backs.

27

Reversible,
gold, human hair on one side,
picture on the other
1870–1885
$450

Mosaic, low karat setting,
1879–1890
$190

Topaz, sapphires, low karat gold,
1870–1880
$350

Rolled gold plate, black enameling,
1880–1890
$85

Low karat gold, black enameling,
1870–1880
$85

Goldstone, low karat gold setting,
1880–1890
$75

Gold plated,
1870–1880
$45

Gold plated, imitation garnets and
sapphire,
1880–1890
$65

Rolled gold plate, blue and black
enameling,
1880–1890
$125

Yellow 14k gold, pearls
$120

Yellow 10k gold, amethyst
$165

Yellow 14k gold, aquamarine
$130

Yellow 10k gold, amethyst
$100

White 10k gold
$125

White 14k gold, blue sapphire
$125

White 10k gold
$100

White 10k gold, blue sapphire
$160

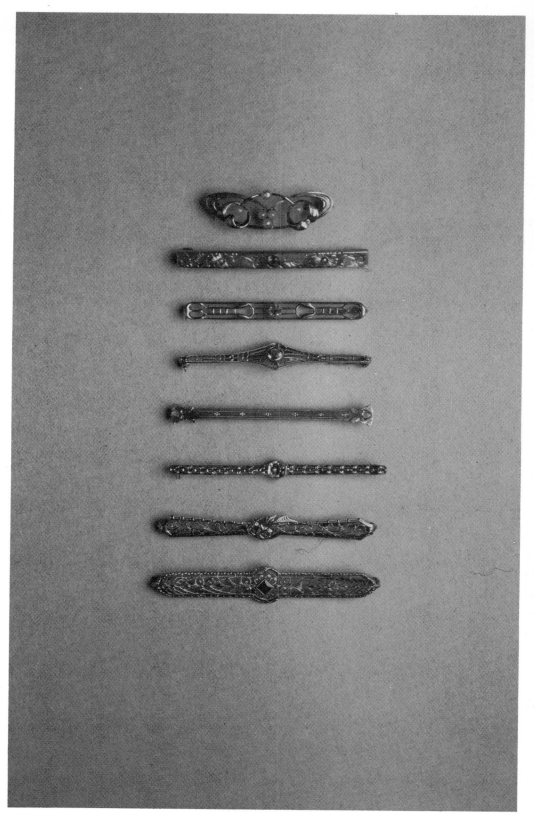

Bar pins, circa 1905–1915.

30

Imitation amethyst,
$35

Imitation amethyst,
$40,

Painted porcelain,
$75

Painted porcelain, tiny imitation
amethysts,
$75

$20

Brooches with gold-plated settings, circa
1900–1920.

Gold filled setting,
1920–1930
$90

Seed pearls
1890–1910
$125

French,
1890–1900
$125

Painted porcelain brooches from varying
periods.

Coral cameo
$150

Branch coral
$85

Coral, black onyx
$85

Branch coral converted to a pendant,
$190

Brooches and earrings, circa 1870–1890,
low karat gold.

Painted porcelain
$45

Painted porcelain
$75

Painted porcelain
$125

Reverse painting on glass
$75

Art Deco brooches, circa 1930, with gold
plated settings.

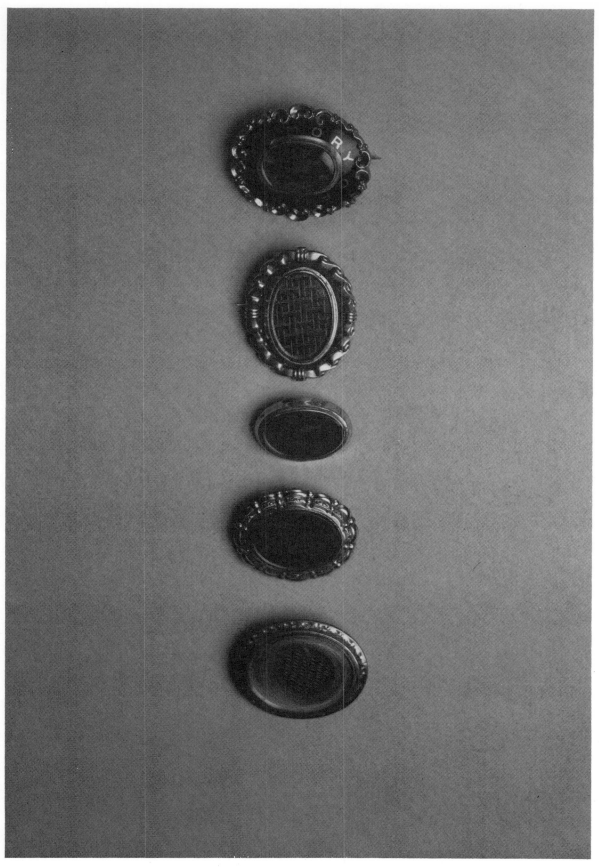

Gold, human hair
1870–1885
$190

Reversible,
gold, human hair
1880–1900
$130

Gold, human hair,
1880–1900
$75

Gold, human hair
1880–1900
$125

Gold, human hair
1880–1900
$95

Goldstone, gold plated
1880–1890
$35

Watch pin,
gold filled
1900–1910
$45

Gold filled
1900–1915
$55

Watch pin,
gold filled
1910–1920
$55

Gold plated
1900–1910
$50

Low karat gold
1890–1900
$75

Turn-of-the-century brooches and watch pins.

Handpainted ivory, sterling setting
$150

Painted ivory, sterling
$150

Painted ivory, sterling
$150

Painted ivory, sterling
$175

Pendant
painted ivory,
sterling with gold plating
$165

Post-1950 brooches and pendant shown are often mistaken for antique jewelry. Such items are readily available in Italy today.

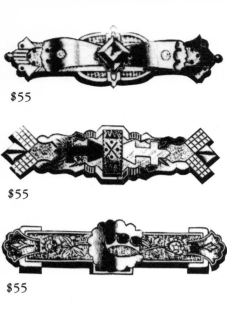

$55

$55

$55

$65

$55

$50

$55

$45

$60

$45

Bar pins, circa 1885, rolled gold plate.

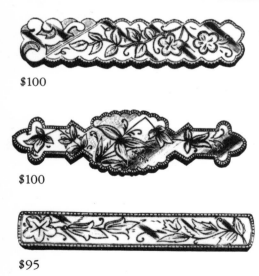

$100

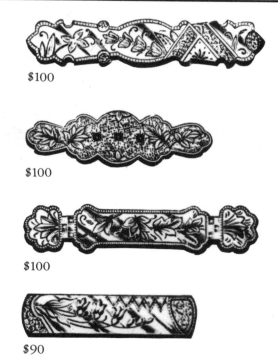

$100

$100

$100

$95

$100

$85

$90

Bar pins, circa 1885, engraved gold fronts.

38

$40 $55 $45 $45

$50 $50 $50 $50

$50 $50 $50 $50

$60 $50 $50 $50

$60 $55 $50

$55 $50 $50 $45

Chatelaine pins, circa 1910. All are $\frac{1}{10}$–14k
gold filled.

Sterling with
non-tarnishable
chromium finish,
one brilliant in
basket setting and
two emeralds
$28

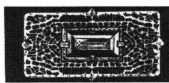

Non-tarnishable
white finish,
light green
imitation olivine
stone
$28

Non-tarnishable
white finish,
two brilliants
and an imitation
zircon
$26

Rhodium, frosted
crystal, one brilliant
imitation onyx
$28

Sterling with
non-tarnishable
chromium finish,
one brilliant in
basket setting
$25

Sterling with
rhodium finish,
imitation crystal and
one brilliant stone
$22

Non-tarnishable
white metal
imitation emerald
$26

Sterling with
enameled center
$26

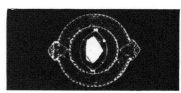

Sterling,
deep green zircon
$26

White 14k gold filled
with rhodium finish,
one brilliant,
imitation crystal, and
onyx
$28

Sterling with
rhodium finish,
five brilliants
$26

Rhodium plated on
white metal, one
brilliant, imitation
crystal
$28

Non-tarnishable
white metal,
imitation amethyst
$24

Sterling with
rhodium finish,
imitation emerald
$22

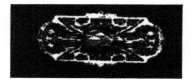

Non-tarnishable
white metal,
light green
imitation emerald
$26

Art Deco brooches, circa 1932.

White 10k gold,
three diamonds
$125

White 10k gold,
one diamond
$100

White 10k gold,
crystal, one
diamond, and black
enameling
$100

White 14k gold,
one diamond
$97

White 14k gold,
one diamond,
four blue sapphires
$140

White 10k gold,
one diamond
$135

White 10k gold,
one diamond,
two sapphires
$159

White 10k gold,
applied 18k red and
green gold flowers,
synthetic Ceylon
sapphire
$150

White 10k gold,
genuine frosted
crystal and one
diamond
$140

White 10k gold,
black onyx and
one diamond
$160

White 10k gold,
applied 18k red and
green gold flowers,
one synthetic emerald
$139

White 10k gold,
applied 18k red and
green gold flowers,
synthetic zircon
$135

White 10k gold,
one diamond,
two blue sapphires
$140

White 10k gold,
one diamond
$140

White 14k gold,
one diamond
$100

White 10k gold,
one diamond and two
heart-shaped sapphires
$170

White 10k gold,
one diamond
$120

White 10k gold,
one diamond,
two emeralds
$160

Art Deco brooches, circa 1932.

$24 $27 $24

$27 $27

$24 $30 $27

$60

$60

Art Moderne sterling brooches and bracelets,
circa 1941.

42

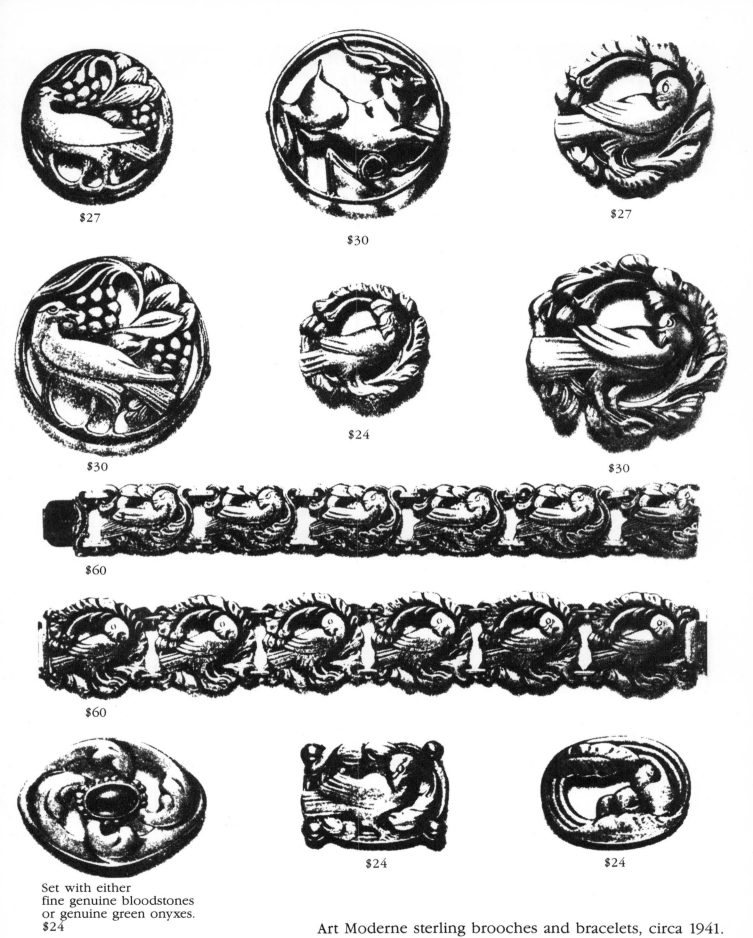

$27

$30

$27

$30

$24

$30

$60

$60

Set with either
fine genuine bloodstones
or genuine green onyxes.
$24

$24

$24

Art Moderne sterling brooches and bracelets, circa 1941.

$30

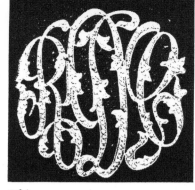

$64

$64

$68

$51

$58

$37

$33

$44

$69

$74

$44

Art Moderne monogram brooches, circa 1941.
All are sterling silver with hand set French
marcasites.

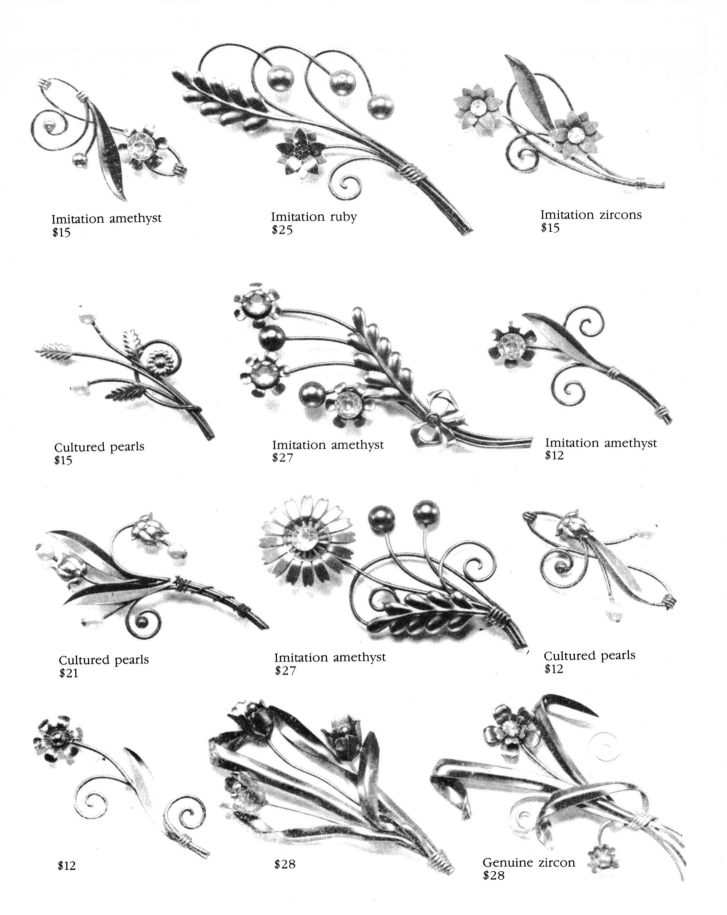

Imitation amethyst
$15

Imitation ruby
$25

Imitation zircons
$15

Cultured pearls
$15

Imitation amethyst
$27

Imitation amethyst
$12

Cultured pearls
$21

Imitation amethyst
$27

Cultured pearls
$12

$12

$28

Genuine zircon
$28

Brooches, circa 1943, gold filled.

Cameo Jewelry

Pendant
Rosalyn shell cameo,
gold filled setting
1900–1920
$95

Brooch-Pendant
Cornelian shell cameo,
low karat gold
1930–1940
$150

Brooch
Yellow 10k gold
sardonyx shell cameo
1935–1945
$165

Pendant
Cornelian shell cameo,
low karat gold setting
1930–1940
$150

Brooch
Cornelian shell cameo,
gold plated setting
Pre–1925
$70

Brooch
Cornelian shell cameo,
gold plated setting
Pre–1925
$85

Cornelian, Rosalyn, and Sardonyx shell
cameo brooches and pendants, circa
1900–1940.

Yellow 10k gold
Rosalyn shell cameo
$195

Yellow 10k gold
Rosalyn shell cameo
$145

Yellow 14k gold
Sardonyx shell cameo
$295

Yellow 10k gold
Sardonyx shell cameo
$195

Yellow 14k gold
Cornelian shell cameo
$225

Shell cameo brooches, circa 1935–1945.

48

Cornelian shell cameo
sterling
$95

Sardonyx shell cameo
sterling
$75

Sardonyx shell cameo
$75

Pictured are three examples of shell cameo
brooches that were made sometime after
1950.

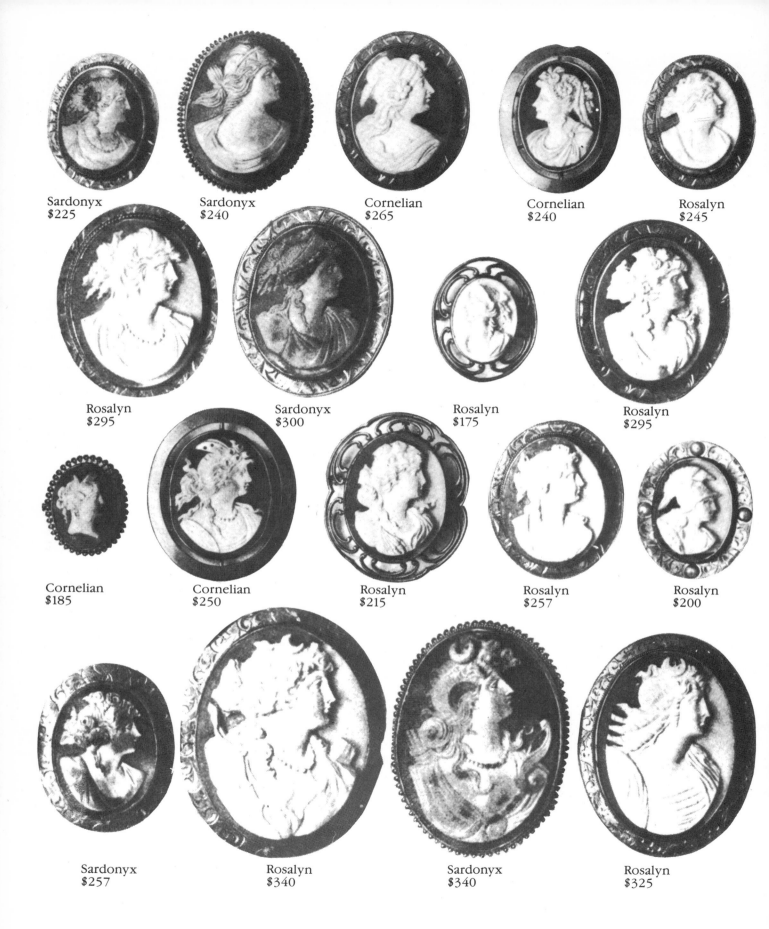

Sardonyx
$225

Sardonyx
$240

Cornelian
$265

Cornelian
$240

Rosalyn
$245

Rosalyn
$295

Sardonyx
$300

Rosalyn
$175

Rosalyn
$295

Cornelian
$185

Cornelian
$250

Rosalyn
$215

Rosalyn
$257

Rosalyn
$200

Sardonyx
$257

Rosalyn
$340

Sardonyx
$340

Rosalyn
$325

Cameo brooches, 10k gold, circa 1913.

White 10k gold,
applied 18k red
and green gold
flowers, cornelian
$185

White 14k gold,
one fine diamond,
cornelian
$145

Yellow 10k gold,
pink rosalyn cameo
has a pendant ring
at top
$140

White 10k gold,
applied 18k red
and green gold
flowers, cornelian
$185

White 10k gold,
cornelian shell
$160

White 14k gold,
cornelian
$135

White 10k gold,
cornelian
$130

Sterling,
cornelian
$150

Sterling,
cornelian,
marcasite frame
$59

Sterling and
chromium,
cornelian, has
pendant ring
$55

White gold plate,
four emeralds,
cornelian
$85

Sterling and
rhodium,
cornelian
$55

Cameo brooches, circa 1932.

Yellow 10k gold,
sardonyx,
cultured pearl
$125

Yellow 10k gold,
cornelian
$75

Yellow 10k gold,
sardonyx,
seed pearl frame
frame
$135

Yellow 10k gold,
cornelian
$90

Yellow 10k gold,
cornelian,
plain frame
$79

Yellow 10k gold,
cornelian,
two-tone frame
$125

Yellow 10k gold,
cornelian,
two diamonds
$160

Yellow 10k gold,
cornelian
$135

Yellow 10k gold,
cornelian,
four diamonds
$160

Yellow 10k gold,
cornelian
$95

Gold filled,
cornelian,
marcasites
$59

Gold filled,
sardonyx,
$49

Gold filled,
cornelian,
$59

Gold filled,
cornelian,
one diamond
$65

Gold filled,
cornelian
$49

Cameo brooches, circa 1941.

Chains and Watches

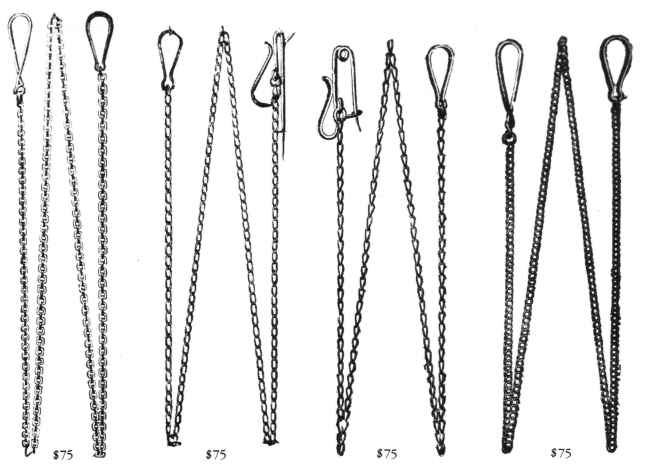

$75 $75 $75 $75

Eyeglass chains, rolled gold plate, circa 1885.

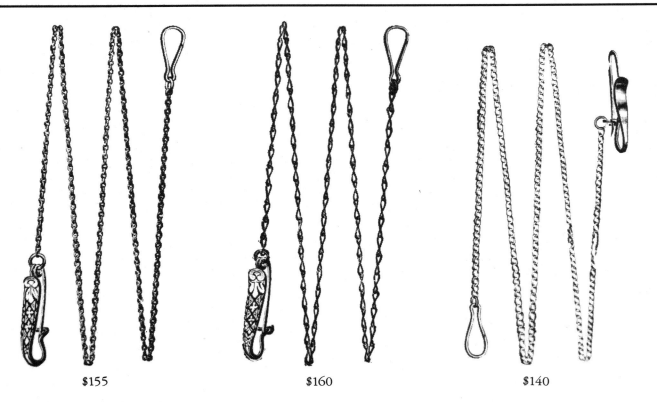

$155 $160 $140

Eyeglass chains, solid gold, circa 1885.

54

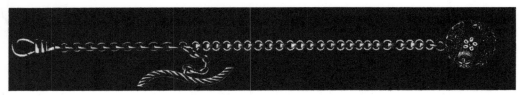

10k chain,
14k charm
$200

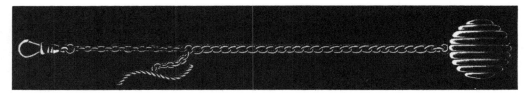

10k chain,
14k charm
$225

10k chain,
14k charm
$200

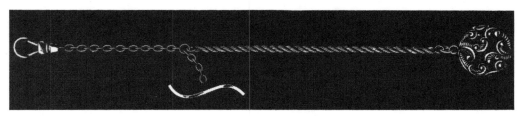

10k chain,
14k charm
$200

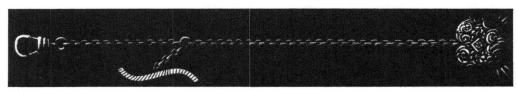

14k chain,
14k charm, diamond
$265

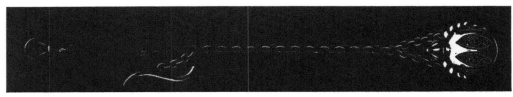

14k chain,
14k charm
$250

Victoria chains, circa 1896.

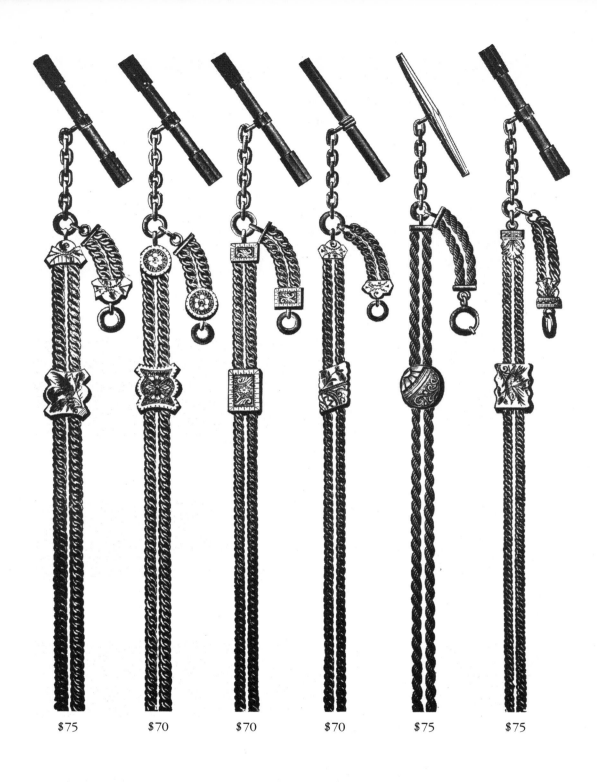

$75 $70 $70 $70 $75 $75

Vest chains, all in rolled gold plate, circa
1896.

$65 $70 $75

Pony vest chains, circa 1896, all rolled gold
plate with sardonyx fobs.

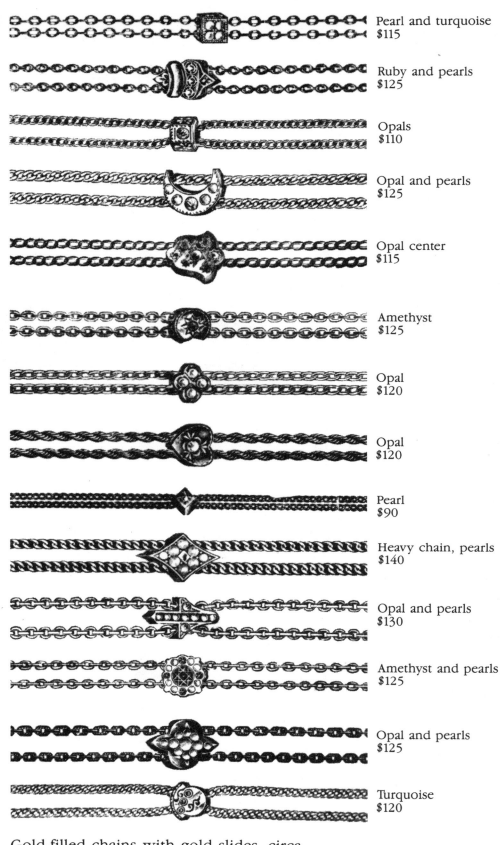

Pearl and turquoise
$115

Ruby and pearls
$125

Opals
$110

Opal and pearls
$125

Opal center
$115

Amethyst
$125

Opal
$120

Opal
$120

Pearl
$90

Heavy chain, pearls
$140

Opal and pearls
$130

Amethyst and pearls
$125

Opal and pearls
$125

Turquoise
$120

Gold-filled chains with gold slides, circa 1902.

Pink and yellow
gold filled,
seven jewel
Rima movement
$80

Yellow 10k rolled
gold plate,
seven jewel
Schwob movement
$67

Cloisonné,
yellow rolled
gold plate
Schwob movement
$67

Gold filled,
seven jewel
Rima movement
$80

Pink and yellow
gold filled,
seven jewel Rima
movement
$80

Pink and yellow
gold filled,
seven jewel Rima
movement
$80

Pink and yellow
gold filled,
seven jewel Rima
movement
$80

Yellow 10k rolled
gold plate,
seven jewel
Schwob movement
$70

Yellow 10k rolled
gold plate and
Lucite, seven
jewel Schwob
movement
$70

Yellow 10k
rolled gold
plate, seven
jewel Schwob
movement
$52

Yellow gold
filled,
seven jewel
Rima Movement
$65

Fob watches, circa 1943.

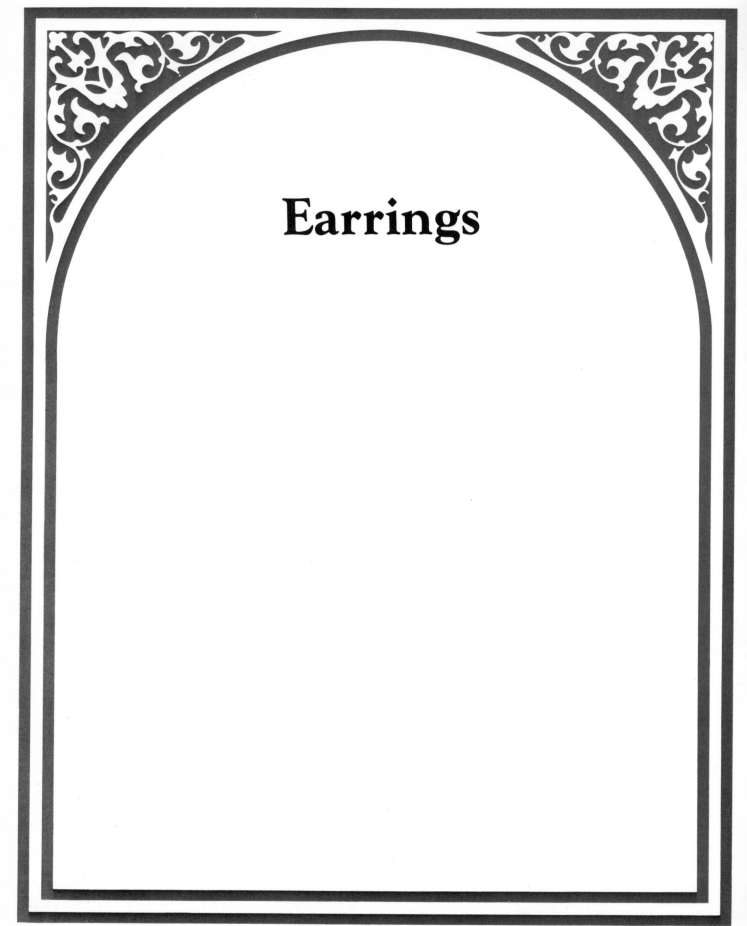

Earrings

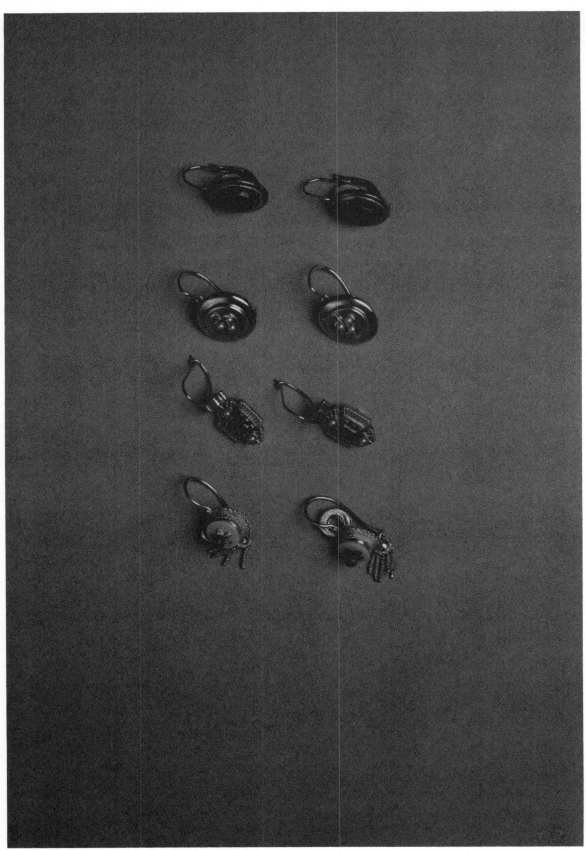

Black enamel
1880–1890
$65

Seed pearls
1880–1890
$74

Imitation garnet,
seed pearls
1890–1900
$75

Coral
1870–1880
$85

Earrings with low karat gold mountings, priced as pairs.

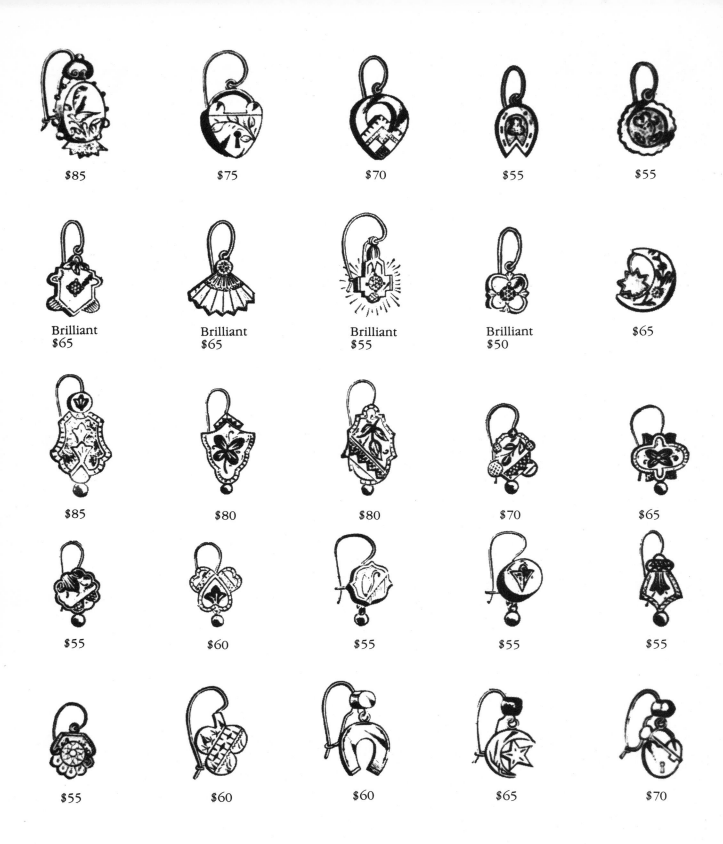

$85 $75 $70 $55 $55

Brilliant   Brilliant   Brilliant   Brilliant $65
$65 $65 $55 $50

$85 $80 $80 $70 $65

$55 $60 $55 $55 $55

$55 $60 $60 $65 $70

Earrings with gold fronts, circa 1880–1890.
These and all other earrings in this book are
priced by the pair.

62

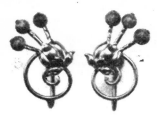

Gold filled,
jade
$12

Cultured pearls,
imitation amethyst,
gold filled
$15

Gold filled,
genuine zircons
$15

Gold filled,
cultured pearls
$12

Gold filled,
imitation amethysts
$12

Gold filled,
imitation amethyst
$10

Gold filled,
cultured pearls
$10

Gold filled
$10

Yellow and red
gold filled
$12

Yellow and red
gold filled
$14

Gold filled,
cultured pearls
$14

Yellow gold filled
$14

Gold filled
$12

Yellow and red
gold filled
$14

Yellow and red
gold filled
$12

Sterling
$10

Sterling
$10

Sterling,
imitation amethysts
$12

Sterling
imitation garnets
$14

Sterling
$12

Sterling
$10

Sterling,
green onyx
$14

Sterling
$12

Sterling,
green onyx
$14

Earrings, circa 1943.

Fobs and
Emblem Charms

Gold filled
1900–1910
$35

1910–1920   1910–1920
$30 $30

1910–1920   1910–1920   Fobs pictured date from the early years of this
$30 $30   century. All, except fob at top are gold plated.

$50 $45 $45 $45 $45

$55 $60 $45 $55 $55

$60 $55 $55 $55 $55

$60 $60 $60 $60 $60

Solid gold charms, circa 1896.

66

$15 $14 $20 $18 $20

$20 $18 $20 $19 $20

$19 $20 $25 $20 $20

$20 $25 $25 $25 $22

Charms, circa 1896, all in rolled gold plate.

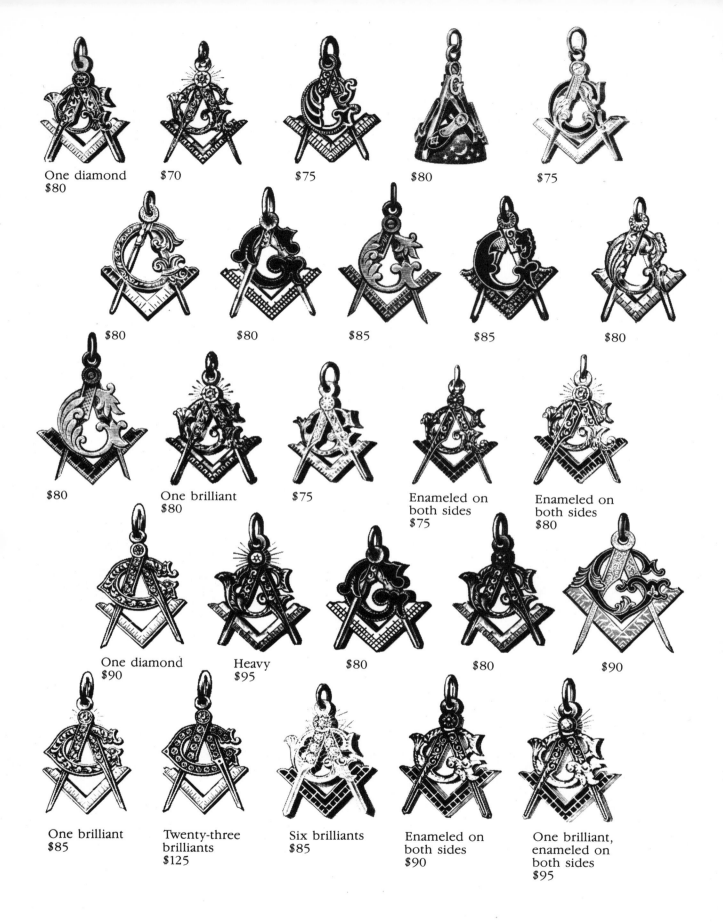

One diamond
$80

$70

$75

$80

$75

$80

$80

$85

$85

$80

$80

One brilliant
$80

$75

Enameled on
both sides
$75

Enameled on
both sides
$80

One diamond
$90

Heavy
$95

$80

$80

$90

One brilliant
$85

Twenty-three
brilliants
$125

Six brilliants
$85

Enameled on
both sides
$90

One brilliant,
enameled on
both sides
$95

Solid gold charms, circa 1917.

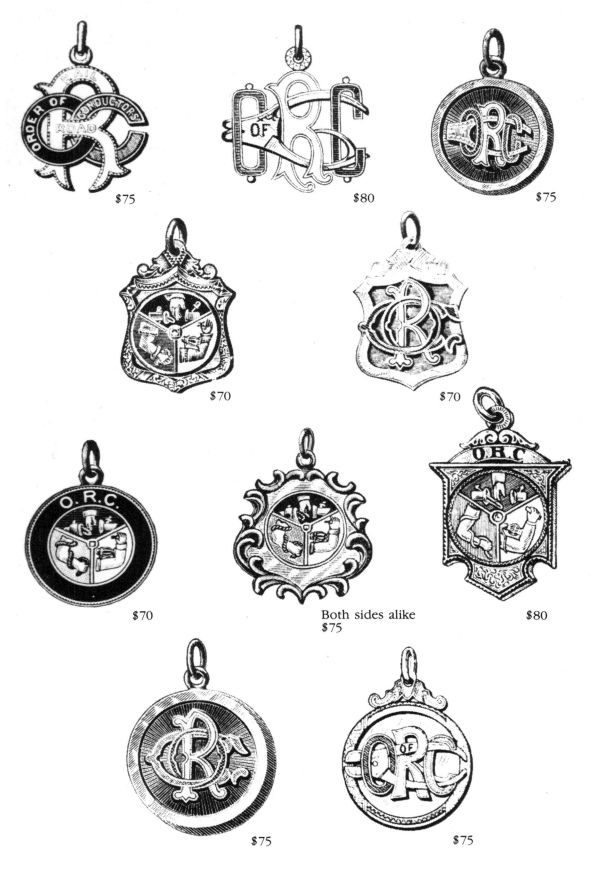

$75

$80

$75

$70

$70

$70

Both sides alike
$75

$80

$75

$75

Emblem charms, Order of Railroad Conductors,
circa 1917, solid gold.

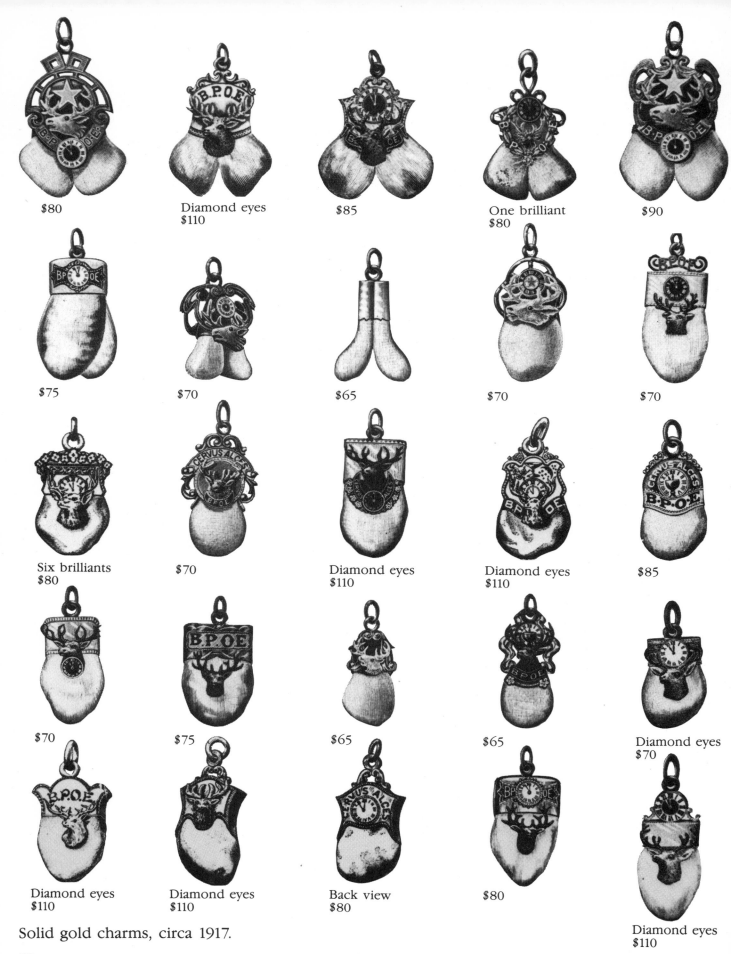

$80

Diamond eyes
$110

$85

One brilliant
$80

$90

$75

$70

$65

$70

$70

Six brilliants
$80

$70

Diamond eyes
$110

Diamond eyes
$110

$85

$70

$75

$65

$65

Diamond eyes
$70

Diamond eyes
$110

Diamond eyes
$110

Back view
$80

$80

Diamond eyes
$110

Solid gold charms, circa 1917.

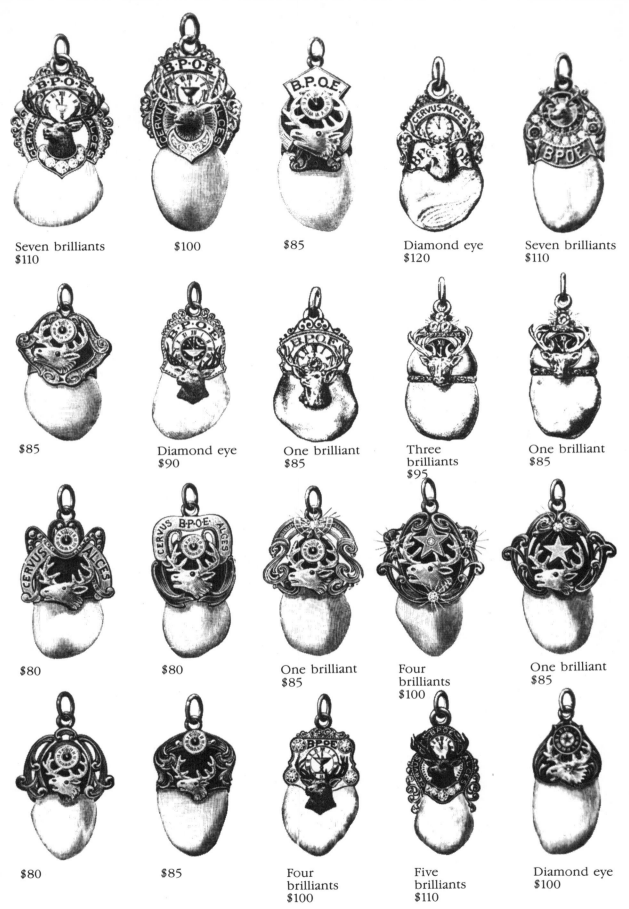

Seven brilliants
$110

$100

$85

Diamond eye
$120

Seven brilliants
$110

$85

Diamond eye
$90

One brilliant
$85

Three
brilliants
$95

One brilliant
$85

$80

$80

One brilliant
$85

Four
brilliants
$100

One brilliant
$85

$80

$85

Four
brilliants
$100

Five
brilliants
$110

Diamond eye
$100

Solid gold charms, circa 1917.

$55 $50 $50 $60 $65

$45 $45 $45 $55 $55

$55 $55 $55 $55 $55

$60 $60 $60 $60 $55

$55 $55 $55 $55 $60

Solid gold fraternal charms, circa 1917.

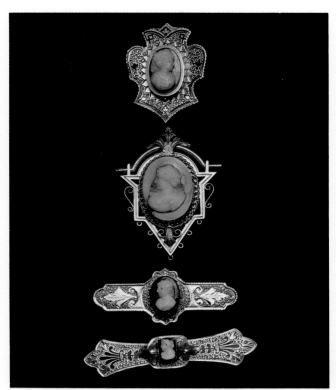

(Top to bottom) Stone cameo brooch, gold front, circa 1860, $225. Stone cameo brooch, gold front, circa 1860, $250. Stone cameo brooch, gold front, circa 1860 $175. Stone cameo brooch, gold front, circa 1860, $175.

(Top to bottom) Child's gold-filled locket, circa 1905, $60. Yellow 10k gold locket with diamond, circa, 1930, $185. Gold-filled locket, circa 1910, $85. Gold-filled moon and star locket with brilliants, circa 1910, $85. Larger gold-filled moon and star locket with brilliants, circa 1910, $125.

(Top to bottom) Bracelet with sterling silver top, circa 1915-1930, $80. Pendant, carved ivory nude, sterling silver, circa 1915, $150. Necklace, 14k gold with platinum overlay, crystal and diamond center, circa 1925, $285.

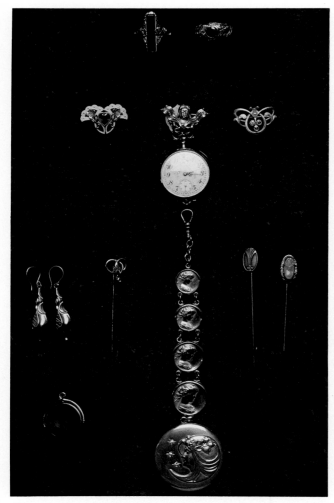

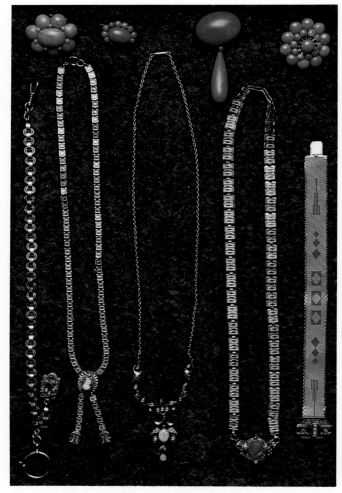

(Row 1, L to R) Ring, banded agate set in white gold, circa 1880, $350. Garnet ring, gold mounting, circa 1880, $375.

(Row 2) Watch pin, 14k gold, three sapphires, one pearl, circa 1900, $175. Watch pin and watch, circa 1900; watch pin, 10k gold, $130; watch, 14k gold, $200. Watch pin, inlaid 10k gold with seed pearls, circa 1900, $145.

(Row 3) Gold-filled earrings, circa 1915, $40. Stickpin, gold filled, circa 1910, $15. Watch chain with locket, both 14k gold, five rose-cut diamonds, circa 1910, $575. Gold-filled stickpin, circa 1910, $20. Gold-filled stickpin, coral setting, circa 1910, $35.

(Row 4) Gold-filled fob, intaglio setting, circa 1910, $45.

(Row 1, L to R) Coral pin, circa 1880, $140. Coral pin, circa 1880, $125. Coral pin with teardrop, circa 1880, $150. Coral pin, circa 1880, $140.

(Row 2) Gold watch chain, circa 1890, $575. Gold-filled cameo necklace, circa 1865-1880, $285. Gold necklace, set with opals, rubies, and pearls, circa 1865-1880, $600. Gold-filled necklace with coral cameo, circa 1865-1880, $325. Bracelet, 14k gold set with pearls, circa 1865-1880, $475.

(Row 1, L to R) Gold-filled earrings, circa 1880, $85. Gold-filled earrings, circa 1880, $85.

(Row 2) Gold-filled pin with mosaic set in goldstone, circa 1880, $185. Locket 14k gold, circa 1880, $300.

(Row 3) Gold-filled pin, circa 1880, $95. Pin, 14k gold, circa 1880, $200.

(Row 4) Watch 14k rose gold with cameo slide, circa 1890, $425. Sardonyx fob with intaglio setting, circa 1895, $85. Gold-filled necklace, circa 1880, $80. Gold fob, circa 1895, $80. Enameled watch with seed pearls, circa 1880, $295.

(Row 1, L to R) Ring, sterling with marcasites and black onyx, $80. Ring, 14k white gold, onyx with crystal diamond chip, $190. Ring, sterling with marcasites and green onyx, $80. Ring, sterling with marcasites and synthetic amethyst, $80. Ring, 14k gold with rubies and diamonds, $395.

(Row 2) Necklace, 14k gold, circa 1935, $150. Pendant-brooch, 14k gold with diamonds and sapphires, circa 1930, $175. Necklace-watch, 10k gold with diamond, black enamel, Swiss movement, circa 1930, $285. Sterling earrings with marcasites and onyx, circa 1935, $59. Necklace, 14k gold with diamond, circa 1935, $175.

(Row 3) Bracelet, 14k white gold, circa 1935, $375.

(Row 4) Bracelet, 14k white gold, circa 1935, $350.

(Row 1, L to R) Lorgnette, 14k gold, circa 1890, $750. Eyeglass case, 14k gold, alligator skin, circa 1900, $1,800. Money clip, 14k gold, ruby eye, circa 1905, $450.
(Row 2) Mesh pocketbook, 18k gold, circa 1905, $1,600. Watch chain, human hair, circa 1890, $150. Handkerchief holder, 14k gold, circa 1890, $350.

(Row 1, top to bottom) Gold watch pin, circa 1900, $155. Gold locket, circa 1870–1890, $390. Gold earrings, circa 1880, $150. Gold brooch with turquoise stones, circa 1880, $140. Gold-filled brooch, banded agate, circa 1860–1890, $95.

(Row 2) Gold necklace, black onyx, gold overlay, circa 1870–1890, $1,800. Gold swivel watch clip, circa 1880, $750.

(Row 3) Gold sardonyx shell cameo brooch, circa 1860–1880, $275. Silver brooch, sardonyx shell cameo, circa 1860–1880, $190. Gold cornelian shell cameo brooch, circa 1880–1900, $190. Painted porcelain brooch, sterling mounting, circa 1895, $90. Cornelian shell cameo brooch, gold-filled mounting, circa 1875, $175.

(Row 1, L to R) Slide chain, 14k gold, circa 1870-1890, $350. Slide chain and gold-filled locket with sardonyx inlay, $190. Bracelet, turquoise and seed pearls, gold mounting, circa 1880-1900, $425. Bracelet, turquoise and seed pearls, gold mounting, circa 1880-1890, $425.

(Row 2, top to bottom) Man's gold Elgin watch and chain, gold fob with bloodstone intaglio, circa 1890-1900, $750. Brooch, gold-filled, human hair, circa 1870-1890, $90. Earrings, gold-filled, circa 1870-1890, $80.

(Row 1, L to R) Ring, garnet set in gold, $225. Ring, garnet and seed pearls in gold, $350. Ring, garnets and seed pearls in gold, $375. Ring, garnet set in gold, $250.

(Row 2) Earrings, garnets, gold filled, $175. Necklace, garnets, gilded silver, $650. Stickpin, garnets, gold filled, $100.

(Row 3) Brooch, garnets set in gilded silver, $125. Fan-shaped brooch, garnets set in gilded silver, $175.

(Row 4) Bracelet, garnets set in brass, $455. All Victorian jewelry pictured above, circa 1880-1890.

(Row 1) Lady's watch, rose-cut diamonds, red and green enameled 18k gold, circa 1895-1915, $1,400.

(Row 2, L to R) Watch and slide, 14k gold, gold filled chain, circa 1890-1910, $475. Watch, 14k gold, circa 1890-1910, $550. Watch and chain, 14k gold watch, 10k gold chain, circa 1890-1910, $485.

(Row 1, L to R) Ring, turquoise and seed pearls, 14k gold, $275. Ring, onyx, cameo, $375. Ring, turquoise and seed pearls, 10k gold, $250.

(Row 2) Ring, tiger eye, intaglio, $300. Ring, tiny rose-cut diamond, amethyst, gold inlay, 14k gold, $395.

(Row 3) Ring, cameo and seed pearls, 10k gold, $375. Ring, sardonyx, rose-cut diamond, 10k gold, $350. Ring, two rose-cut diamonds, black onyx with gold inlay, 10k gold, $350. All rings pictured above, circa 1870-1890.

Genuine elk tooth $85

Genuine elk tooth $80

Genuine elk tooth $80

Genuine elk tooth $75

Genuine elk tooth $75

Genuine elk tooth $80

Genuine elk tooth $75

Genuine elk tooth $80

Genuine elk tooth $80

Genuine elk tooth $80

Genuine elk tooth $75

Genuine elk tooth $75

Genuine elk tooth $65

Genuine elk tooth $65

Genuine elk tooth $70

Genuine elk tooth $70

Genuine elk tooth $80

$55

$55

$55

$55

$55

$60

$55

$55

Solid gold B.P.O.E. charms, circa 1917.

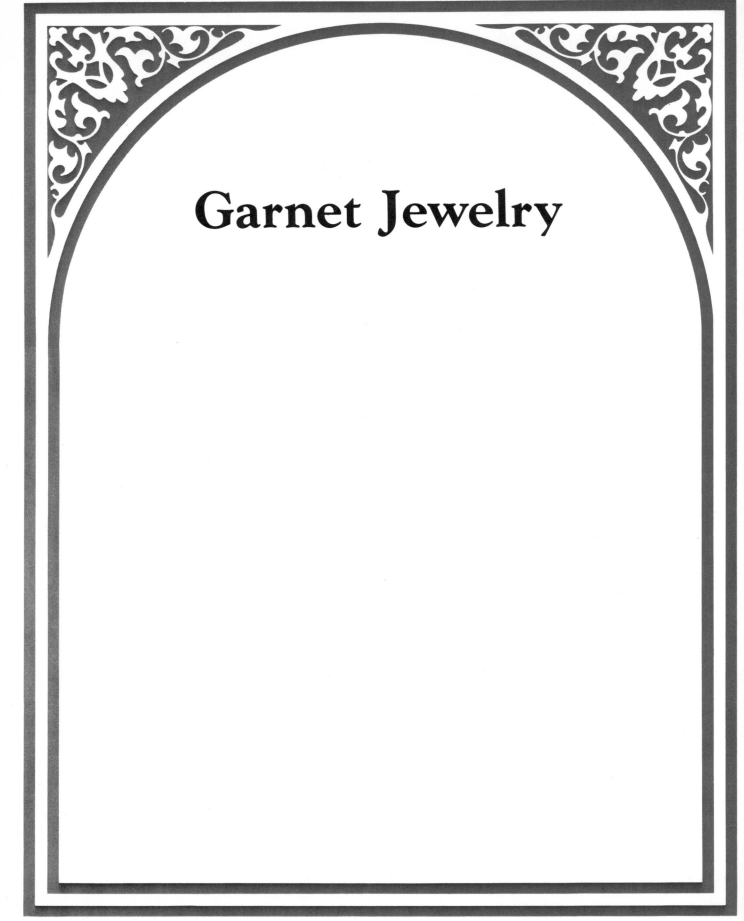

Garnet Jewelry

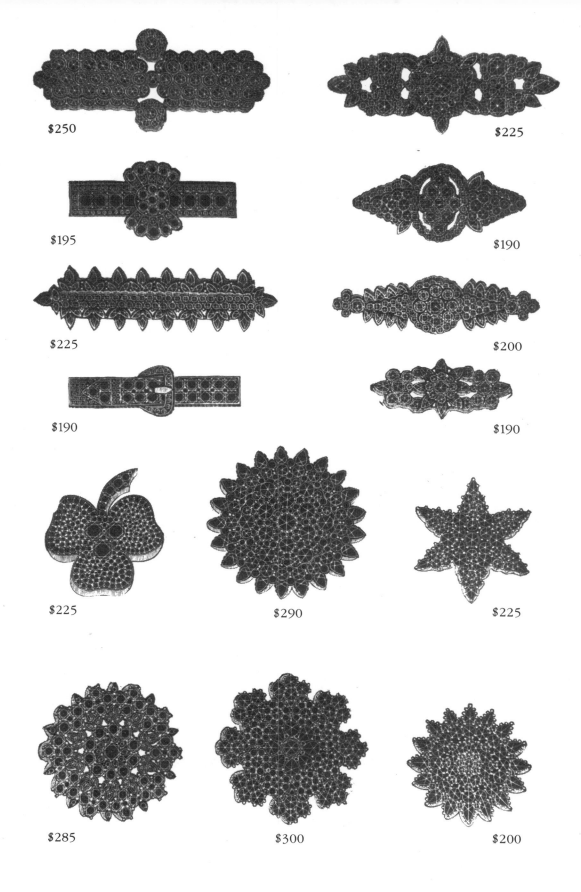

$250

$225

$195

$190

$225

$200

$190

$190

$225

$290

$225

$285

$300

$200

Bohemian garnet brooches with gold mountings,
circa 1889.

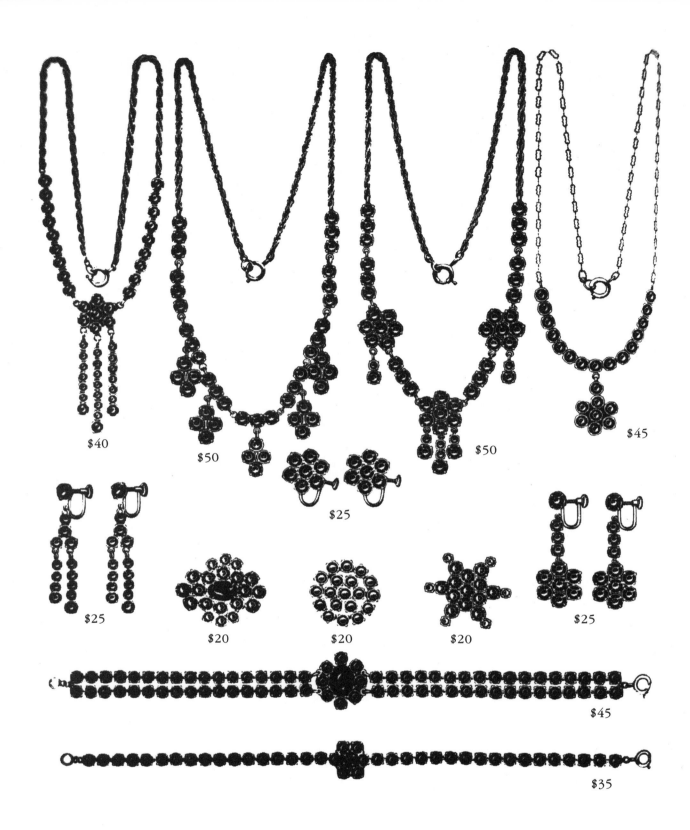

$40

$50

$50

$45

$25

$25

$20 $20 $20 $25

$45

$35

Imitation garnet jewelry in gold plated settings,
circa 1932.

Lavaliers, Lockets, Necklaces, and Pendants

$250 $195

Victorian gold filled cameo necklaces, circa
1870–1890.

1870–1885
$80

1870–1880
$75

1890–1900
$85

Pendant,
coral
1865–1875
$90

Gold plated lockets and pendant, dating from circa 1865 to circa 1900.

Circa 1940
Imitation diamond
$75

Circa 1930
Cornelian cameo
$85

Circa 1930
Gold filled
$85

Gold filled lockets from the 1930s and 1940s.

$75

$85 $95

Gold filled lockets, circa 1900-1915; stones are brilliants.

Imitation topaz
$60

Pale blue enameled locket
$65

Imitation amethyst
$85

Sterling silver necklaces, circa 1930-1940. Top and bottom necklaces are rhodium-plated to prevent tarnishing.

Mine cut diamonds
1870–1880
$275

Onyx
1890–1900
$125

Black enameling
1870–1880
$150

Modern spring ring
Victorian period,
seed pearls
$195

Opal
1890–1900
$185

Lockets with low karat gold mountings.

Painted porcelain front, back
1890–1900
$190

1895–1910
$250

Pendant
Post–1925
Limoges porcelain
$85

Painted porcelain lockets and pendant with low
karat gold mountings.

92

$35

Ruby,
white stones
$40

$35

$35

Ruby, sapphire,
white stone
$45

$30

$30

$35

Enameled
$35

$30

$30

$35

White stone
$35

White stones
$35

White stones
$35

White stone
$35

Ruby,
white stone
$40

White stone
$35

$30

$30

White stones
$35

$30

$30

Emerald and
white stones
$40

Emerald and
white stones
$40

Gold-filled lockets, circa 1896.

93

Turquoise
$110

$110

Turquoise
$125

Brilliants
$110

Brilliants
$110

$95

Brilliants
$125

$110

$110

Gold-filled lockets, circa 1907.

$80 $70 $75 $80

$75 $75 $75 $95 $75

$75 $75 $75 $80

$65 $80 $75 $80 $80

$90 $85 $85 $80

$70 $80 $65 $65 $75

$75 $65 $80 $75

Gold-filled lockets set with brilliants, circa
1905–1915.

95

Two
diamonds
$175

Two
diamonds
$160

Diamond,
baroque
pearls
$150

Diamond,
baroque
pearls
$150

Diamond,
pearls
$155

Two
diamonds
$165

Two
pearls,
two
diamonds
$155

Diamond,
pearls
$160

Diamond,
pearls
$165

Two
diamonds
$175

Pearls,
diamond
$160

Pearls,
diamond
$150

Three
diamonds
$180

Diamond
pearls,
sapphire
$180

Pearls,
sapphire
$160

Pearls,
sapphire
$165

Diamond
$160

Pearl,
sapphire,
diamond
$165

Pearls,
sapphire,
$155

Pearls,
sapphire,
diamond
$175

Lavaliers mounted in 14k gold, circa 1913.

Sapphires, pearls
$145

Diamond,
baroque pearls
$150

Diamond, two
sapphires, and pearls
$145

Diamond
$135

Diamond, sapphire,
and pearls
$140

Diamond,
baroque pearl
$140

Sapphire,
baroque pearl
$140

Diamond, pearls
$210

Imitation amethyst,
baroque pearls
$140

Diamond,
amethysts, pearls
$150

Sapphire and pearls
$145

Gold filigree
$135

Diamond,
baroque pearls,
and pearls
$150

Gold filigree,
amethyst bands
$150

Sapphire, diamond, and
pearls
$155

Imitation amethyst,
pearls
$145

Lavaliers mounted in 10k gold, circa 1913.

Sterling,
marcasites
$53

Sterling,
marcasites
$53

Sterling,
marcasites,
and chrysoprase
$58

Sterling,
marcasites,
and chrysoprase
$58

Sterling,
marcasites,
and black onyx
$54

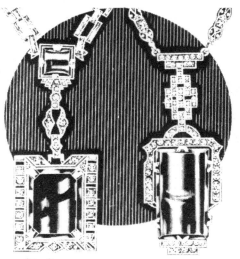

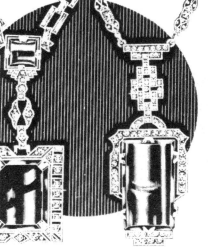

Sterling,
marcasites,
and black
onyx
$56

Sterling,
marcasites,
and black onyx
$67

Sterling,
marcasites,
and black onyx
$67

Rhodium,
marcasites,
and
imitation
emerald
$60

Sterling,
marcasites,
and
imitation
amethyst
$56

Rhodium,
marcasites,
imitation
pearls, and crystals
$55

Sterling,
marcasites,
and imitation
emerald
$53

Necklaces mounted in sterling or rhodium, circa 1932.

Chrome finish
green onyx
$55

Sterling,
imitation
onyx and
brilliants
$65

Chrome finish,
imitation jet
$45

Rhodium,
marcasite,
and pearl
$40

Green and red
gold filled,
turquoise
$55

Sterling,
frosted crystal,
brilliant
$60

Sterling,
amethyst
$65

Rhodium,
imitation blue
sapphire,
brilliant
$55

Chrome finish,
imitation
zircon
$45

Sterling,
amethyst
$60

Assorted necklaces, circa 1932.

Sterling,
onyx, imitation
crystal,
brilliant
$65

Rhodium,
imitation
crystal,
brilliant
$45

Rhodium,
black onyx,
brilliant,
crystal
$40

Chrome finish
imitation
emerald
$42

Sterling,
brilliant,
imitation
onyx
$60

Rhodium,
brilliant,
imitation
black onyx
$75

Yellow gold
filled,
green stones
$70

White 14k
gold filled,
one brilliant,
two emeralds
$85

Rhodium,
one brilliant
$65

Sterling,
cornelian
shell cameo
$75

Assorted necklaces, circa 1932.

Green 14k
gold,
six genuine
zircons
$145

Yellow 14k
gold,
six diamonds
$175

Yellow 14k
gold,
two genuine
garnets
$155

Yellow 14k
gold,
genuine
zircon
$155

Yellow 14k
gold,
genuine
zircon and
four
diamonds
$160

White 14k
gold,
one diamond
in crystal
$185

Yellow 14k
gold, with
genuine jade
$155

Yellow 14k
gold, with
one diamond
$155

Yellow 10k
gold, blue
green zircon,
and two
diamonds
$140

Yellow 10k
gold,
one diamond
$145

Yellow 10k
gold with
genuine
zircon
$140

Green 14k
gold, jade
$160

Yellow 10k
gold, one
diamond,
cornelian
cameo
$165

Yellow 10k
gold, black
onyx, and
one diamond
$145

Yellow 10k
gold, one
diamond
$145

Yellow 10k
gold,
genuine
zircon
$45

Yellow 10k
gold, one
diamond,
black onyx
$145

Yellow 10k
gold with
cornelian
cameo
$180

Assorted necklaces, circa 1940.

½₂₀–12k
$42

¹⁄₁₀–14k
$45

½₂₀–10k
one diamond
$40

¹⁄₁₀–14k
$45

½₂₀–10k
$40

½₂₀–10k,
cornelian
cameo
$60

½₂₀–12k
$45

½₂₀–10k,
four
photographs
$30

½₂₀–12k
$40

½₂₀–10k
$40

½₂₀–10k
$40

½₂₀–12k,
cornelian
cameo
$55

½₂₀–10k
$40

½₂₀–10k
$35

½₂₀–12k
$45

½₂₀–12k
$35

½₂₀–10k
imitation
turquoise
and pearls
$40

½₂₀–12k
$40

½₂₀–12k
$40

Yellow gold filled lockets, circa 1940. All except
one are designed to hold two photographs.

102

Black enamel
inlay
$32

Engine turned
$21

Black enamel
inlay, four
pictures
$28

Black enamel
inlay, four
pictures
$21

Applied cross,
four pictures
$21

Cornelian
cameo
$75

Cornelian
cameo
$65

Cornelian
cameo
$55

Black onyx,
one fine
diamond
$60

Black and white
enamel
$30

One fine
diamond
$41

Roman finish,
one fine
diamond
$41

Engraved,
one fine
diamond
$45

Engraved,
one fine
diamond
$45

Engraved,
one fine
diamond
$45

One fine
diamond
$36

One fine
diamond
$36

One fine
diamond
$36

Imitation
amethysts
$32

Imitation
garnets
$36

Gold filled lockets, circa 1941. All will hold two
pictures, except three in top row.

103

Bright
finish
$120

Bright
finish
$85

Black onyx,
one diamond
$125

Embossed,
engraved
$90

Embossed,
engraved
$100

Bright
finish
$120

Bright
finish
$85

Roman
finish
$100

Roman
finish
$100

Roman
finish
$100

Bright
finish
$125

Roman
finish
$135

Engraved
$40

Engraved
$35

Engraved
$30

Embossed,
engraved
$45

Embossed,
engraved
$40

Cornelian
cameo
$60

Engine
turned
$29

Black onyx
$35

Cornelian
cameo
$30

Black
enamel
$34

Engine
turned
$19

Engraved
$23

Two-picture lockets, circa 1941. Top two rows are all 10k yellow gold. Last two lockets in bottom row are sterling silver; remainder are gold filled.

104

Miscellaneous

$80 $90 $75

$75 $70 $80 $55

$140 $190 $225 $250

Selection of gold crosses, circa 1880–1890.
Top and center rows: rolled gold plate. Bottom
row examples are all solid gold.

Mourning Jewelry

Carved jet brooch
$95

Carved jet earrings
$100

French jet (black glass)
cameo brooch
$165

Mourning brooch,
gold, black enamel, hair
$130

Mourning brooch,
gilt, black enamel, hair
$100

Jet jewelry, circa 1850–1880.

Jet, rolled gold
plated trim
$45

Jet, rolled gold
plated trim
$40

Jet, rolled gold
plated trim
$40

Jet, rolled gold
plated trim
$40

Jet, rolled gold
plated trim
$40

Jet, rolled gold
plated trim
$40

Jet, crepe finish
$50

Jet, crepe finish
$50

Jet, crepe finish
$50

Jet, crepe finish
$50

Jet, crepe finish
$50
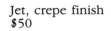

Jet, crepe finish
$50

Onyx, gold trim
$95
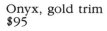

Onyx, gold trim
$85

Onyx, gold trim
$90

Onyx, gold trim
$70

Onyx, gold trim
$95

Onyx, gold trim
$95

Onyx, gold trim
$75

Onyx, gold trim
$85

Selection of bar pins, circa 1889.

Pendant
$150

Locket
$185

Locket
$185

Locket
$210

Carved jet pendant and lockets, circa 1860–1880.

French jet,
cut and polished,
gilt scroll,
plaited hair
$140

Carved bog oak
$150

Dark tortoiseshell,
gold and silver initials,
hair
$75

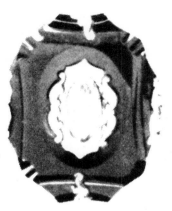

French jet,
gold frame,
plaited hair
$120

Carved bog oak
$180

Gilt and black enamel,
hair
$110

Brooches and crosses, circa 1850–1870.

Rings

White 18k gold
with diamonds
$1,200

White 14k gold
with diamonds
$900

Platinum and
diamonds
$4,000

Pink 10k gold
with six synthetic
rubies
$165

Pink 10k gold
with four
synthetic rubies
$155

Pink 10k gold,
synthetic rubies
$175

Yellow 10k gold,
genuine opal,
six synthetic rubies
$170

Pink 10k gold
with three synthetic
rubies, three pearls
$150

Pink 10k gold,
genuine rubies
and diamonds
$400

Rings, circa 1930–1940.

Opals, garnets
and pearls
$110

Artificial
oriental
pearls
$85

Emerald and
twenty pearls
$150

Opals,
emeralds,
and pearls
$110

Three opals,
eight pearls
$85

Artificial
pink pearls
$85

Pearls,
emeralds, and
rubies
$160

Opals, pearls,
amethysts
$125

Two rubies,
three opals
$100

Three garnets,
two pearls
$90

Opal
$90

Opal
$90

One ruby,
twenty-four
pearls
$115

Opal and
amethyst
$175

Garnet
$115

Ruby
$90

Three opals,
six pearls
$85

Two rubies,
five pearls
$90

Four opals,
nine
pearls
$95

Emeralds,
rubies, pearls
$100

Three rubies,
six pearls
$125

Turquoise,
pearls
$90

Three amethysts,
six pearls
$125

Two opals,
three rubies,
twelve pearls
$110

Opal,
six rubies,
$135

Two rubies
$115

Ruby, pearls
$125

Pearl,
amethyst
$110

Artificial
pearls
$85

Opal,
twelve pearls
$150

Opal
$100

Opal,
two rubies
$110

Three opals
$115

Bloodstone
$85

Opal
$115

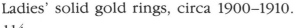

Ladies' solid gold rings, circa 1900–1910.

114

Green 10k gold
$180

White 10k gold
$110

Green 14k gold
$190

Green 10k gold
$160

Green 10k gold
$95

White 18k gold,
black onyx,
one diamond
$195

White 18k gold,
black onyx,
one diamond
$150

White 14k gold,
one diamond
$145

White 18k gold,
black onyx
$165

Green 10k gold
$90

White 14k gold,
black onyx,
one diamond
$250

White 10k gold,
six diamonds
$180

White 10k gold,
six diamonds,
onyx
$225

Yellow 10k gold,
six diamonds,
black onyx
$225

White 10k gold,
six diamonds,
black onyx
$225

White 14k gold,
black onyx
$175

Green 14k gold,
black onyx
$160

White 10k gold,
one diamond,
black onyx
$150

Green 10k gold,
black onyx
$175

White 10k gold,
black onyx
$160

Men's rings, circa 1932.

Marcasites,
hematite
$70

Marcasites,
hematite
$60

Marcasites,
crystal
$60

Marcasites,
black onyx
$60

Marcasites,
black onyx
$50

Marcasites,
black onyx
$60

Marcasites,
black onyx
$60

Marcasites,
black onyx
$70

Marcasites,
black onyx
$40

Marcasites,
black onyx
$55

Reversible,
green
synthetic
zircon,
onyx,
one diamond
$160

Reversible,
onyx,
cornelian
cameo,
$185

Reversible,
onyx,
diamond,
cameo,
$185

Onyx,
diamond,
cameo,
diamond
$195

Reversible,
cameo,
diamond,
crystal,
$275

Reversible,
onyx,
diamond,
crystal,
$275

Cameo,
crystal,
diamond
$175

Ruby,
diamond,
crystal,
diamond
$225

Onyx with
diamond,
synthetic ruby
$155

Onyx,
diamond,
genuine
amethyst
$175

Onyx with
diamond,
cameo
$165

Cameo,
diamond,
onyx,
$250

Cameo,
diamond,
four
aquamarines
$285

Ladies' rings, circa 1932. Top two rows have
sterling silver mountings. Four necklaces and remainder of rings are mounted in 14k white gold.

Aquamarine
$175

Deep amethyst
$180

Aquamarine
$175

Amethyst
$180

Synthetic
emerald
$130

Amethyst
$180

Topaz
$150

Brilliant black
opal
$140

One diamond,
black onyx
$185

Two diamonds,
aquamarine
$190

One diamond,
four aquamarines
$185

Black onyx,
one diamond
$195

Two diamonds,
aquamarine
$195

Two diamonds,
aquamarine
$195

Two diamonds,
aquamarine
$195

Two diamonds,
aquamarine
$195

Black onyx,
one diamond
$170

Black onyx,
one diamond
$175

Black onyx,
two diamonds
$180

Black onyx,
one diamond
$195

Men's fraternal rings, circa 1932, mounted in 14k
white gold.

| 14k, diamond $190 | 14k, diamond $190 | Diamond $180 | 14k $175 | 14k, diamond $190 |

Diamond $175   Black onyx, two diamonds $180   14k $160   Diamond $175   Synthetic sapphire $150

Black onyx $160   Black onyx $160 $150   Synthetic blue spinel $145   Black onyx $160

Black onyx $160   Diamond, ruby eyes $175   14k $170   14k $165   Black enamel $165

Black onyx $140   14k, one diamond, five synthetic stones $135   Black onyx $150   Enameling $135   Black onyx $135

Men's fraternal rings, circa 1940. Most are mounted in 10k yellow gold. Seven have 14k yellow gold mountings and are so identified.

14k,
black onyx,
one diamond
$160

14k,
black onyx,
three diamonds,
$175

14k
black onyx,
seven diamonds,
$210

14k,
black onyx,
five diamonds,
$190

14k,
black onyx
one diamond
$155

Black onyx,
one diamond
$150

Black onyx,
one diamond
$150

Black onyx,
one diamond
$150

Black onyx,
one diamond
$165

Black onyx
$155

14k,
cornelian
cameo
$165

Cornelian
cameo
$150

One diamond,
cornelian
cameo
$160

Opal
$160

Opal
$175

Hematite
intaglio,
two diamonds
$155

Tiger eye cameo
$145

Tiger eye cameo
$145

Hematite
intaglio
$140

Black onyx
intaglio
$150

Ladies' rings, circa 1940, in 10k yellow gold
mountings unless otherwise identified.

Red gold trim,
four
synthetic
rubies
$190

Genuine
zircon
$170

Red gold trim,
three
synthetic
rubies
$190

Red,
white gold
trim
$180

Genuine
zircon
$170

Genuine
amethyst
$185

Red,
yellow gold
trim
$160

Red gold trim,
genuine zircon
$170

Genuine
zircon
$165

Red
gold trim
$165

Genuine
amethyst
$175

Red gold
trim,
genuine
zircon
$185

Red
gold trim
$160

Red gold trim,
genuine
zircon
$175

Red gold
trim,
genuine
amethyst
$165

Ladies' rings, circa 1942, all mounted in 14k
yellow gold.

Bibliography

Catalogs

Busiest House in America, Illustrated Catalogue of Watches, Jewelry, Silverware, Clocks, Canes, Umbrellas, 1889.

Fort Dearborn Watch and Clock Co., Illustrated Fort Dearborn Gift Book and General Catalog. Chicago, 1932.

Gatter, R.S. Jewelry of the Better Sort, New York: R.S. Gatter, 1910.

R.H. Mach and Co., No. 17, 1911.

H.M. Manheim and Co., New York, 1941.

H.M. Manheim and Co., New York, 1942.

H.M. Manheim and Co., New York, 1943.

L.C. Mayers Co. 1940. Fifth Avenue, New York.

Marshall Field and Co., Illustrated Catalogue of Jewelry and Fashions, Chicago, 1896.

Montgomery Ward and Co., 1902–1903.

J.W. Richardson & Co., Illustrated Catalogue of Solid Gold Emblems, New York, 1917–1918.

Sears, Roebuck and Co., Fall 1900.

Sears, Roebuck and Co., Best of Sears Collectibles 1905–1910.

Sears, Roebuck and Co., 1923.

Books

Baker, Lillian. *100 Years of Collectible Jewelry.* Paducah, Kentucky: Collector Books, 1978.

Baker, Lillian. *Art Nouveau and Art Deco Jewelry.* Paducah, Kentucky: Collector Books, 1981.

Bell, Jeanenne. *Old Jewelry.* Florence, Alabama: Books Americana, Inc., 1982.

Branson, Oscar. *What You Need To Know About Gold and Silver.* Tuscon, Arizona: Treasure Chest Publications Inc., 1980.

Cooper, Diana. Battershill, Norman. *Victorian Sentimental Jewellery.* Cranbury, New Jersey: A.S. Barnes & Co., Inc., 1973.

Curran, Mona. *Collecting Antique Jewellery.* New York, N.Y.: Emerson Books, Inc., 1970.

Curran, Mona. *A Treasury of Jewels and Gems.* New York, N.Y.: Emerson Books, Inc., 1962.

Darling, Ada W. *Antique Jewelry Identification,* Des Moines, Iowa: Wallace-Homestead Book Co., 1973.

Darling, Ada W. *The Jeweled Trail.* Des Moines, Iowa: Wallace-Homestead Book Co., 1971.

Darling, Ada. *Antique Jewelry Identification.* Leon, Iowa: Mid-America Book Co., 1967.

Desautels, Paul E. *The Gem Kingdom.* New York, N.Y.: Random House The Ridge Press Inc., 1971

Dickinson, Joan Younger. *The Book of Diamonds.* New York, N.Y.: Avenel Books, 1965.

Flower, Margaret. *Victorian Jewellery.* Cranbury, New Jersey: A.S. Barnes and Co., Inc., 1967.

Gere, Charlotte. *Victorian Jewelry Design.* Chicago, Illinois: Henry Regnery Co., 1972.

Goldemberg, Rose, Leiman. *Antique Jewelry: A Practical and Passionate Guide.* New York, N.Y.: Crown Publishers, Inc., 1976.

Harris, Nathaniel. *Victorian Antiques.* London, England: Hampton House Productions Ltd., 1973.

Hayes, Maggie. *Maggie Hayes Jewelry Book.* New York, Cincinnati, Toronto, London, Melbourne: Van Nostrand Reinhold Company, 1972.

Henzel, Sylvia S. *Old Costume Jewelry: A Collector's Dream.* Des Moines, Iowa: Wallace-Homestead Book Co., 1978.

Lewis, M.D.S. *Antique Paste Jewellery.* Boston, Massachusetts: Boston Book and Art, 1970.

Mason, Anita. *An Illustrated Dictionary of Jewellery.* Wallop, Hampshire, Great Britain: Osprey Publishing Limited, 1973.

Mebane, John. *What's New That's Old.* Cranbury, New Jersey: A.S. Barnes and Co., Inc., 1969.

Mebane, John. *The Complete Book of Collecting Art Nouveau.* New York, N.Y.: Weathervane Books, 1970.

Meyer, Florence E. *Pins for Hats and Cravats,* Des Moines, Iowa: Wallace-Homestead Book Co., 1974.

McClinton, Katharine Morrison. *Antiques Past and Present.* New York, N.Y.: Clarkson N. Potter, Inc., 1971.

Nijssen, L. Giltay. *Jewelry.* New York, N.Y.: Universe Books, Inc., 1964.

Norbury, James. *The World of Victoriana.* London, New York, Sydney, Toronto, Middlesex, England: The Hamlyn Publishing Group Limited, 1972.

Revi, Albert, Christian. *The Spinning Wheel's Complete Book of Antiques,* New York, N.Y.: Grosset and Dunlap, 1977.

Sallee, Lynn. *Old Costume Jewelry.* Florence, Alabama: Books Americana, Inc., 1979.

Vandergroot, R.L. *Facets of Wealth.* Scottsdale, Arizona: Palladian House, 1976.

Whitlock, Herbert P. *The Story of the Gems.* New York, N.Y.: Emerson Books, Inc., 1970.

Index

Bracelets
bangle, 8, 10, 12, 14
bride's, 8
cameo, 9, 12
cuff, 17
garnet, 8, 79, 84
expansion, 15, 18
heart charm, 19
heart lock, 11
link, 13, 16, 20, 73, 75
sterling, 42, 43
woven mesh, 16, 74, 78

Brooches and pins
Art Deco, 40, 41
Art Moderne, 42, 43, 44
banded agate, 77
bar pins, 22, 30, 38, 109
buckle, 31
cameo, 25, 33, 47, 48, 49, 50, 51, 52, 73, 77
chatelaine (watch), 24, 36, 39, 74, 77
coral, 33, 74
floral, 45
garnet, 79, 83, 84
hair, 25, 28, 35, 78, 108, 111
hollowware, 23
jet, 108, 109, 111
marcasite, 44
mosaic, 26, 28, 75
painted ivory, 37
painted porcelain, 26, 27, 32, 34, 77
reverse painting
    on glass, 34
reversible, 35
sterling, 42, 43, 77
stickpins, 74, 79
white gold filigree,

Chains
eyeglass, 54
pony vest, 57
slide, 58, 75, 78, 80
vest, 56
victoria chain, 55
watch, 59, 74, 75, 76, 78, 80

Crosses
enameled, 29
gold, 106
hair, 25
mourning, 111

Earrings, 33, 61, 62, 63, 74, 75, 77, 78, 79, 84, 108

Emblem charms and fobs,
B.P.O.E., 81
fraternal, 72
Order of Railroad Conductors, 69

Eyeglass case, 76

Handkerchief holder, 76

Intaglios, 25, 74, 75, 78, 80, 119

Lavaliers, 96, 97

Lockets, 18, 73, 74, 75, 77, 78, 88, 89, 91, 92, 93, 94, 95, 102, 103, 104, 110

Lorgnette, 76

Mesh pocket book, 76

Money clip, 76

Necklaces, 73, 74, 75, 77, 79, 84, 86, 90, 98, 99, 100, 101

Pendants, 37, 47, 73, 75, 87, 92, 110

Rings
banded agate, 74
emblem, 115
cameo, 80, 116. 119
fraternal, 117, 118
garnet, 74, 79
ladies', 114, 116, 119, 120
marcasite, 75, 116
miscellaneous, 80, 113
tiger eye intaglio, 80

Watches, 74, 75, 78, 80

About the Author

Doris Jean Snell is a multitalented, hardworking author who has utilized extensive research experience to produce six books about American silverplated flatware and this one about antique and collectible jewelry.

Mrs. Snell graduated from Gettysburg College, attended medical school, worked in medical research and, in later years, developed and wrote Medicaid regulations for the Pennsylvania Department of Public Welfare. When her son died in 1980 she retired and since that time she has been operating a shop in her home and participating in many antique shows.

Over the past twenty-five years Mrs. Snell has amassed large collections of silver, jewelry, autographs of famous persons, and other paper items of historical nature. In fact, her collection of paper Americana may very well be one of the largest on the eastern seaboard. Favored leisure pursuits of this busy lady include travel and musical composition.